Women employees at an aviation plant in Long Beach, California, polish lines of transparent noses for A-20 attack bombers. During the War years more than three million women found work in war-related jobs on the home front.

THE HOME FRONT: U.S.A.

WORLD WAR II · TIME-LIFE BOOKS · ALEXANDRIA, VIRGINIA

BY RONALD H. BAILEY

AND THE EDITORS OF TIME-LIFE BOOKS

THE HOME FRONT: U.S.A.

Time-Life Books Inc.
is a wholly owned subsidiary of
TIME INCORPORATED

Founder: Henry R. Luce 1898-1967

Editor-in-Chief: Henry Anatole Grunwald
President: J. Richard Munro
Chairman of the Board: Ralph P. Davidson
Executive Vice President: Clifford J. Grum
Chairman, Executive Committee: James R. Shepley
Editorial Director: Ralph Graves
Vice Chairman: Arthur Temple

TIME-LIFE BOOKS INC.

Managing Editor: Jerry Korn
Executive Editor: David Maness
Assistant Managing Editors: Dale M. Brown
(planning) George Constable, Thomas H. Flaherty Jr.
(acting), Martin Mann, John Paul Porter
Art Director: Tom Suzuki
Chief of Research: David L. Harrison
Director of Photography: Robert G. Mason
Assistant Art Director: Arnold C. Holeywell
Assistant Chief of Research: Carolyn L. Sackett
Assistant Director of Photography: Dolores A. Littles

Chairman: Joan D. Manley
President: John D. McSweeney
Executive Vice Presidents: Carl G. Jaeger,
John Steven Maxwell, David J. Walsh
Vice Presidents: George Artandi (comptroller);
Stephen L. Bair (legal counsel); Peter G. Barnes;
Nicholas Benton (public relations); John L. Canova;
Beatrice T. Dobie (personnel); Carol Flaumenhaft
(consumer affairs); James L. Mercer (Europe/South
Pacific); Herbert Sorkin (production);
Paul R. Stewart (marketing)

WORLD WAR II

Editorial Staff for *The Home Front: U.S.A.*
Editor: William K. Goolrick
Picture Editor/Designer: Raymond Ripper
Text Editors: Jim Hicks, Anne Horan
Staff Writers: Dalton Delan, Richard W. Flanagan,
Henry Woodhead
Researchers: Martin Baldessari,
Michael Blumenthal, Oobie Gleysteen,
Karen L. Michell, Clara Nicolai, Phyllis K. Wise,
Frances G. Youssef
Editorial Assistants: Dolores Morrissy,
Connie Strawbridge

Editorial Production
Production Editor: Douglas B. Graham
Operations Manager: Gennaro C. Esposito,
Gordon E. Buck (assistant)
Assistant Production Editor: Feliciano Madrid
Quality Control: Robert L. Young (director),
James J. Cox (assistant), Daniel J. McSweeney,
Michael G. Wight (associates)
Art Coordinator: Anne B. Landry
Copy Staff: Susan B. Galloway (chief), Victoria Lee,
Barbara F. Quarmby, Celia Beattie
Picture Department: Alvin L. Ferrell
Traffic: Jeanne Potter

Correspondents: Elisabeth Kraemer (Bonn);
Margot Hapgood, Dorothy Bacon, Lesley Coleman
(London); Susan Jonas, Lucy T. Voulgaris (New
York); Maria Vincenza Aloisi, Josephine du Brusle
(Paris); Ann Natanson (Rome). Valuable assistance
was also provided by: Enid Farmer (Boston);
Donna Miskin (Chicago); Jean Belden (Houston);
Judy Aspinall, Karin B. Pearce (London);
Carolyn T. Chubet, Miriam Hsia, Christina
Lieberman (New York); Mimi Murphy (Rome);
Robert Case (Waterloo, Iowa).

The Author: RONALD H. BAILEY is a freelance author and journalist who was formerly a senior editor of *Life.* He is the author of *Violence and Aggression* and *The Role of the Brain* in Time-Life Books' Human Behavior series, and has written a photography book, *The Photographic Illusion: Duane Michals.* He has also published several articles on prison reform for the magazine *Corrections* and was a contributor to *The Unknown Leonardo,* a book about the inventive genius of Leonardo da Vinci. While at *Life,* he edited a book of Larry Burrows' war photographs, *Larry Burrows: Compassionate Photographer.*

The Consultants: COLONEL JOHN R. ELTING, USA (Ret.), is a military historian and author of *The Battle of Bunker's Hill, The Battles of Saratoga* and *Military History and Atlas of the Napoleonic Wars.* He edited *Military Uniforms in America: The Era of the American Revolution, 1755-1795* and *Military Uniforms in America: Years of Growth, 1796-1851,* and was associate editor of *The West Point Atlas of American Wars.*

RICHARD POLENBERG, Professor of American History at Cornell University, is the author of *Reorganizing Roosevelt's Government, 1936-1939* and *War and Society: The United States, 1941-1945,* and is the co-author of *The American Century,* a history of the United States in the 20th Century. He was the editor of *America at War: The Home Front* and *Radicalism and Reform in the New Deal.*

For information about any Time-Life book, please write:

Reader Information
Time-Life Books
541 North Fairbanks Court
Chicago, Illinois 60611

CONTENTS

THE JITTERY HOMELAND

A few days after Pearl Harbor, a hastily constructed barrier of sandbags protects the telephone company in San Francisco against bombs that never came.

GETTING READY FOR THE LONG HAUL

On December 7, 1941, thirteen-year-old Douglas Jaynes heard the news of the sneak attack on the radio and raced through the streets of Florence, Alabama, to spread the word to the neighbors. "The Japs have bombed Pearl Harbor," shouted the self-appointed town crier, "and they're headed for us on Four Mile Creek." This youthful distortion of geography, which had the enemy making a waterborne assault down a tributary of the Tennessee River, reflected the worst fears of citizens of more advanced years.

In practically every city and village in the nation, Americans felt threatened. In Georgia, a citizen's army known as the State Guard—those too young or too old for the draft and others with deferments—set about preparing coastal defenses for an anticipated German invasion. To meet the emergency, Georgia convicts were conscripted and put to work round-the-clock in an effort to improve seashore approaches and build bridges over which the home-grown army would rush to meet the invaders on the beaches. In the landlocked state of Arizona, far removed from the Atlantic or the Pacific oceans, residents fretted over the prospect of trouble from another direction. "We've got the Mexican border to worry about," one said. "Things are liable to pop down there any time." The top officer of the American Legion in Wisconsin appealed for the creation of a guerrilla army that would be composed of the state's 25,000 licensed deer hunters—"a formidable foe for any attackers," he insisted.

Almost everywhere, the preparations to repulse the enemy were tinged with fear and panic. In San Francisco, a sentry on the Bay Bridge shot and seriously wounded a woman motorist who was slow to halt at a checkpoint. In Los Angeles, an antiaircraft battery blazed away against imaginary warplanes; the shell fragments descended on the city, injuring dozens of the jittery residents. But as the nation spent a subdued Christmas season and the new year arrived without an enemy attack, frayed nerves calmed somewhat and Americans settled into a stringent wartime routine marked by shortages, rationing and dimouts.

Anticipating a wartime shortage of alcohol, Washington, D.C., shoppers jam the Milstone's Acme Liquor store in the Christmas season of 1941.

Chomping a cigar, national Price Administrator Leon Henderson pedals a "Victory" bicycle—touted as a wartime stand-in for automobiles—in January 1942.

ON THE ALERT AFTER PEARL HARBOR

In the confusion that came on the heels of Pearl Harbor, the frenzied behavior of the American people took some bizarre and even irrational turns. Air-raid alarms—every one false—and accompanying blackouts threw major cities into panic.

In Seattle, during one of the frequent air-raid alerts, a mob of 1,000 angry citizens attempted to enforce the blackout by smashing windows and looting stores that did not comply with the lights-out order. One skeptic in San Francisco, fed up with incessant sirens, asked a valid question: "If there are Jap planes around why aren't they dropping bombs?" The next morning, Lieut. General John L. DeWitt, the chief of the West Coast defenses, insisted against all evidence that 30 enemy warplanes had flown over San Francisco. "Why bombs were not dropped, I do not know," he said. "It might have been better if some bombs had dropped to awaken this city."

In New York, where officials decided that the schools would close in the event of an air-raid alert, a false alarm released one million children from their classrooms and sent distraught parents through the streets in search of their kids.

A New York cop protects Japanese diplomat Morito Morishima outside the consulate on December 7.

A Coast Guard motor lifeboat escorts San Francisco crab fishermen in early 1942, a time when the West Coast feared attacks from Japanese submarines.

Dug into a California beach in December 1941, a soldier trains his machine gun seaward while his buddy shovels sod on top of their well-lighted gun nest.

In an experiment inspired by the Army, steel mills in Gary, Indiana, test a dense smoke screen designed to conceal factories from the eyes of enemy pilots.

PRECAUTIONS PEOPLE TOOK

Although the possibility of invasion or attack by an enemy many miles away was remote, America took no chances. While preparations comforted some people, they made others anxious, and the strident pronouncements by officials did little to calm their fears. "This is war," declared General DeWitt. "Death and destruction may come from the skies at any moment." On the East Coast, Mayor Fiorello La Guardia predicted that New York would be attacked. "The war will come right to our cities and residential districts," he warned. "Never underestimate the strength, the cruelty of the enemy."

Gun emplacements sprouted overnight on rooftops in the major cities and along the seashores of both coasts. Searchlights danced in the night skies, seeking enemy warplanes. Even in sparsely populated Wyoming, which would hardly have been a high-priority enemy target, a group of nervous citizens called for the construction of bomb shelters, and others eyed caves and mine shafts as places of refuge in case of enemy attack.

No hamlet was too isolated and no city was too sophisticated to completely escape the post-Pearl Harbor jitters. Americans fretted, tacked black cloth on their windows and waited, half-expecting their homeland to be tested by the fires of war.

A model couple in a government photo demonstrate the correct way to tack up a blackout curtain.

Air-raid wardens smoke under a streetlamp where match-striking was allowed in the first blackouts.

An Army sentinel stands guard on a rock overlooking the Potomac River near Washington, D.C., in the early weeks of the War when the nation's capital kept an especially close watch for saboteurs. With the Washington Monument for a backdrop (right), an antiaircraft gunnery crew on the roof of the Commerce Building maintains a vigil for enemy warplanes.

1

All week long the weather had been so unseasonably warm that in New England the pussy willows suddenly budded, and residents began twisting them into special Christmas wreaths. For most Americans, it promised to be the brightest Christmas season in a decade. Europe and parts of Asia had been at war for more than two years, but Americans had not really felt the impact of the fighting. The peacetime draft and the gradual shift to defense production were putting people back to work after years of Depression unemployment, and direct involvement in the War still seemed remote. President Franklin D. Roosevelt had repeatedly promised American mothers, "Your boys are not going to be sent into any foreign wars."

On Manhattan's Fifth Avenue, where double-decker buses were packed with Christmas shoppers, store windows featured the very latest in expensive fashions—calf-length dresses with shoulder pads. Across the land, consumers with new cash in their pockets crowded into movie theaters to watch Greta Garbo in *Two-Faced Woman* or bought radios and hummed the new hit song "I Don't Want to Set the World on Fire."

Sunday, December 7, 1941, was the final day of the professional football season and in Washington, D.C.'s Griffith Stadium 27,102 spectators were watching quarterback Sammy Baugh lead the hometown Redskins to a 20-14 victory over the Philadelphia Eagles. Midway in the first quarter, a series of puzzling announcements crackled over the public-address system. "Admiral W. H. P. Blandy is asked to report to his office at once," the voice on the loudspeaker said. Soon the Philippine commissioner to the United States was being paged, and then others—newspaper editors, the superintendent of police, key Army and Navy officers—were called.

As more and more VIPs were summoned over the loudspeaker, the ball park hummed with excitement. On the Eagle bench, sportscaster Lindsey Nelson, then a young Army second lieutenant, was watching the game as the guest of three former college classmates who played for Philadelphia. "Along the bench and in the stands," he later recalled, "people began to whisper, 'What's this all about? What's happening?' "

Up in the stands, a young Navy ensign named John Fitzgerald Kennedy was enjoying the game; he did not learn

A DAY TO REMEMBER

the reason for the announcements until he turned on his car radio on the way home. In the office of the stadium owner, Clark Griffith, a telephone call came through between halves, and Congressman Joe Martin, the Republican Minority Leader of the House of Representatives, who was chatting with Griffith, immediately rushed back to the Capitol. The assistant director of the Federal Bureau of Investigation, Edward Tamm, viewing the game from a box seat, was called to a special three-way telephone hookup. At one end was his boss, J. Edgar Hoover, who was spending the weekend in New York. At the other end was the FBI's chief agent in Honolulu, who was holding the mouthpiece of the phone near the open window of his office. Thus, echoing faintly across 5,000 miles, the explosions of Japanese bombs rocking the U.S. Naval base at Pearl Harbor reached the ears of America's top two G-men.

The bombs were still falling when the stunning news reached most Americans via radio. Millions were listening to the Columbia Broadcasting System that afternoon when, just as the New York Philharmonic was tuning up for Shostakovich's Symphony No. 1, John Daly's familiar voice broke in a few minutes after 3 p.m.: "We interrupt this program to bring you a special news bulletin. The Japanese have attacked Pearl Harbor."

Though the attack proved to be the worst military disaster in U.S. history—five battleships sunk or beached, three others damaged, 10 smaller warships knocked out, some 2,400 American servicemen dead—the listeners did not yet know its full tragic dimensions. What stunned them was the suddenness and sneakiness of it: an attack on a peaceful Sunday, against a place many people had never heard of.

Of all the momentous events that would galvanize their lives over the next four years, this was the one that Americans would remember most vividly. It was as if a camera had suddenly clicked in their minds and frozen in place every motion and thought at the instant when they heard the news of the attack.

There were 120 million Americans who were old enough to grasp the significance of what was happening, and each reacted in his own particular way, mixing astonishment, outrage and disbelief with his own particular concerns.

At Fort Sam Houston, Texas, a temporary brigadier general named Dwight David Eisenhower was trying to catch up on his sleep after weeks of exhausting field maneuvers when the telephone awoke him. He took in the news, then ran toward the front door, dressing as he went and yelling over his shoulder to his wife, Mamie, that he did not know when he would be back. The novelist John Steinbeck, visiting in New York, wondered what would happen to his Japanese gardener back home in California. In New Jersey an old man, remembering how, three years before, Orson Welles had panicked listeners with his radio fantasy about an invasion from Mars, cackled: "Ha! You got me on that Martian stunt! I had a hunch you'd try it again!" In San Antonio, in a scene that must have been repeated in many forms, a young couple had just finished a family quarrel when newscaster H. V. Kaltenborn's war bulletin on NBC brought them together again, holding hands as they listened to his broadcast.

Richard M. Nixon, a young lawyer who had been thinking about applying for a government job, heard the news as he left a movie theater in Los Angeles. Being a Quaker, Nixon wondered whether he could actually kill an enemy. Jackie Robinson, the all-around athlete who later was to shatter precedent by becoming the first black man to break the color barrier in baseball's major leagues, was on his way back to California aboard the liner *Lurline,* after a season of professional football in Hawaii. Robinson first became aware that something extraordinary had happened when members of the crew began racing around the ship, painting the porthole windows black and passing out life jackets to the passengers.

In Pittsburgh, the isolationist Senator Gerald Nye of North Dakota was telling 2,500 enthusiasts at an America First rally why the nation ought to stay out of foreign wars when a reporter sent him a note about Pearl Harbor. "It sounds terribly fishy to me," Nye remarked. And in Washington, another isolationist leader, Senator Arthur Vandenberg of Michigan, was in his bedroom pasting into a scrapbook newspaper clippings about his long fight to keep America out of the War. Now, with America actively involved, he immediately phoned the White House to assure President Roosevelt of his support.

In that moment of shock and anguish, friend and foe alike turned to the White House. Crowds gathered almost immediately on the sidewalk by the Pennsylvania Avenue entrance, milling around in silence, waiting perhaps for a glimpse of the famous Roosevelt grin or the reassuring sound of the cultivated accent that many had mocked. One woman, who walked to the White House from a nearby movie theater, remembered later that her legs carried her there as if by "homing instinct."

The nation's hopes were now embodied in the man in a wheel chair, the commander in chief of a country under attack. Fortunately, the President was an irrepressible spirit who seemed to thrive on adversity. At 39 he had survived an attack of infantile paralysis. "If you have spent two years in bed trying to wiggle your big toe," he once remarked, "everything else seems easy." The only thing Roosevelt feared was fire—and that only because he was crippled.

December 7 had started routinely for him. He had spent a quiet but painful morning having his balky sinuses treated by his personal physician, Commander Ross T. McIntire. Then, after begging off from a luncheon with his wife, Eleanor, who was entertaining 30 guests in the Blue Room, he ate his midday meal with Harry Hopkins in his second-floor office, hoping to catch up afterwards on his stamp collection. Hopkins was the President's most trusted adviser, a pinched-faced iconoclast whose powers were such that many of his detractors referred to him as "the assistant President." He was lolling on a sofa, eating from a tray, talking with the President—as he was later to recall—about "things far removed from war." The President, wearing a pull-over sweater with the sleeves pushed up, sat at his desk while his Scottish terrier, Fala, raced back and forth between the two men, begging tidbits from them.

In a short while Secretary of State Cordell Hull was scheduled to meet with two Japanese diplomats, Admiral Kichisaburo Nomura, the Ambassador to the United States, and Saburo Kurusu, a special representative of the Japanese Premier. A large Japanese convoy of warships and troopships was now known to be on the move in the South China Sea. An attack appeared imminent somewhere in Southeast Asia: perhaps against Thailand, Malaya, the Dutch East Indies or the Philippines. Intense negotiations between the United States and Japan had been going on during the past month. Now, at noon on December 7—a Sunday—the Japanese Ambassador had called to request a 1 o'clock meeting with the Secretary of State. It was apparent that a showdown was at hand.

The President let Hull handle the meeting, and had left word with the switchboard that he did not want to be disturbed. But around 1:40 p.m. the phone rang in his office. The operator, begging his pardon, said that Secretary of the Navy Frank Knox insisted upon speaking with the President. A bluff former Chicago newspaper publisher, Knox had boasted only three days previously at a dinner party with the Vice President and other notables that, "No matter what happens, the U.S. Navy is not going to be caught napping."

Roosevelt put down the apple he was munching and listened as Knox said, "Mr. President, it looks like the Japanese have attacked Pearl Harbor."

Roosevelt gasped: "No!"

Knox read him a signal that he had received from Naval headquarters in Honolulu: "Air raid on Pearl Harbor. This is not a drill."

Roosevelt was stunned and angered by the news. Hopkins suggested there might be some mistake. But Roosevelt thought the report probably was true. It was just the sort of thing he expected from the Japanese—striking without warning at the least expected place.

Leaving his apple unfinished and putting momentary hesitation behind him, the President swung into action as Commander in Chief. Barking orders into the phone like the captain on the bridge of a ship, he summoned the Secretaries of State, War and Navy and the Army Chief of Staff, General George C. Marshall, who had just returned from a horseback ride to the site where the new Pentagon was to be built. Hopkins watched and later noted in his diary that Roosevelt seemed thankful that the enemy had "made the decision for him." Now the momentous question of whether the U.S. should intervene in the War was entirely out of his hands.

When Roosevelt dialed Cordell Hull's coded number at the State Department, the two Japanese envoys were already waiting in the outer office to see the Secretary. The President told Hull to go ahead and receive them formally and coolly, then bow them out.

The Japanese diplomats wore formal morning coats and striped pants, and when Hull sternly ushered them into his

The day after Pearl Harbor, a tense President Roosevelt (top right) asks Congress to declare war on Japan. In the background, Vice President Henry Wallace and Speaker of the House Sam Rayburn listen somberly; son James Roosevelt is at the President's left. The brief speech—less than 500 words—was broadcast around the country and heard by millions of Americans, including the crowd (right) gathered beside a car radio in front of the Treasury Building on New York's Wall Street.

office at 2:20 p.m. they smiled and bowed stiffly. The two men looked like caricatures of punctilious diplomats, and in the American wartime imagination they came to symbolize the perfidy of the Japanese—smiling in Washington while their countrymen were bombing Pearl Harbor.

The Japanese envoys were not aware that Pearl Harbor was to be attacked—indeed, was being attacked even as they delivered their government's latest written message. But Hull, a Tennessean with the temper and vocabulary of a mule skinner, did know it. He also knew the substance of the message that Nomura and Kurusu were now bringing with them. The Japanese had decided that there was no hope of peace and were breaking off their negotiations with the United States. Like all of the important diplomatic messages that had been sent by the Japanese during the past year, it had been intercepted and deciphered by American cryptanalysts. The intercepts were code-named "Magic," and Hull had been reading them for more than a year. Hull listened impatiently to the envoys, making them stand like schoolboys in front of his broad mahogany desk, then lecturing and dismissing them at approximately 2:30 p.m. When they were out of earshot he exploded, denouncing them as "piss-ants."

Meanwhile, at the White House, Roosevelt phoned his press secretary, Steve Early, who had been at home relaxing in his pajamas and reading the Sunday newspapers. "Have you got a pencil handy, Steve?" asked the President. Early, thinking his boss was playing some joke, asked: "Do I need it?" Roosevelt dictated to him a press release about Pearl Harbor. Then, at 2:20 p.m., Early was linked by a special telephone hookup to the three major wire services in Washington, D.C.—the Associated Press, United Press and International News Service. At UP, a reporter named Arthur F. DeGreve listened to Early, then slammed down the phone and rang up Phil Newsom on the news desk of his New York headquarters.

"This is DeGreve in Washington!" he shouted. "Flash! White House announces Japanese bombing Wahoo!"

"Bombing what?"

"Wahoo, dammit! *Wahoo!*"

"Spell it, for Pete's sake."

"O-A-H-U—Wahoo! We got a war on our hands!"

By 3 o'clock Roosevelt was conferring with his top mili-

tary advisers and issuing a flurry of orders. He flung them out one after another in rapid fire, saying that he would make them legal later by signing the proper Executive Orders. He ordered protection for all military bases, munitions factories and major bridges, as well as for the Japanese Embassy in Washington and Japanese consulates across the country. The President also directed the Federal Bureau of Investigation to round up Japanese aliens who were considered a threat to national security. He grounded all private planes and silenced amateur radio operators.

Both at home and abroad, the armed forces of the United States were put on emergency alert. Their numbers were large according to peacetime standards—some 2.1 million men—but they were untested, ill trained and poorly equipped. In recent maneuvers, many servicemen had carried dummy rifles, lobbed eggs instead of hand grenades and practiced artillery fire with log cannon. Soldiers who quickly took up posts at key government buildings in Washington, D.C., wore World War I helmets and carried World War I Springfield rifles.

Millions of Americans expected the mainland of the United States to be invaded at any moment after the attack on Pearl Harbor. One hysterical government official called the White House to say that, since the Pacific Coast was no longer defensible, new defense lines would have to be

Japanese diplomats Saburo Kurusu (on the left) and Kichisaburo Nomura are all smiles as they leave the State Department following a peace conference with Secretary Cordell Hull 17 days before the attack on Pearl Harbor. After war was declared, the two were sent to Japan in exchange for American Ambassador Joseph C. Grew and the members of his staff.

drawn up in the Rocky Mountains. In Athol, Massachusetts, across the fields from historic Concord, a group of modern minutemen oiled up their shotguns and squirrel rifles and began holding military drills. On Whidbey Island in Puget Sound, Washington, farmers armed with pitchforks, shotguns and clubs patrolled up and down the beaches.

At the White House the fear of invasion was coupled with anxiety for the safety of the President. As Michael Reilly, Roosevelt's personal bodyguard, later recalled, Secretary of the Treasury Henry Morgenthau Jr. phoned and "screamed as though stabbed," ordering him to double the contingent of Secret Service agents around the President. Ten seconds later, Morgenthau called back and ordered Reilly to quadruple the guard.

Machine-gun emplacements were set up on the roof of the White House. Contingency plans were drawn for infantrymen to be rushed in from nearby Fort Meyer, Virginia, in case of attack. Army engineers with bulldozers and other heavy equipment were assigned to the task of freeing casualties from the wreckage in case the White House was bombed. At a secret airstrip on the edge of Washington, an Army Air Forces bomber was kept warmed up so that the President could if necessary be whisked away from Washington. Roosevelt was issued a gas mask, which he slung over his wheel chair.

In the basement of the White House, Army engineers began marking off the entry for a tunnel leading beneath East Executive Avenue to a temporary Presidential bomb shelter in the old vaults under the Treasury building. Roosevelt hated the idea of holing up there and told Treasury Secretary Morgenthau he would use the shelter only if he could play poker with the nation's hoard of gold. The President balked outright at another suggested war measure: the Army proposed painting the White House black. He did not object to normal blackout precautions, however, and shortly after the attack was announced, his housekeeper, Henrietta Nesbitt, began taking measurements for blackout curtains for each of the Executive Mansion's 60 rooms and 20 baths.

On the night of December 7, as a misty three-quarter moon hung over the darkened White House, approximately one thousand people gathered along Pennsylvania Avenue and across the street in Lafayette Park to watch the stream of Cabinet officers and congressmen arriving at the Executive Mansion. At one point, the spectators broke into a ragged chorus of patriotic songs, including "The Star-Spangled Banner" and "God Bless America." In spite of all that had happened during the day, their mood was confident. Their optimism and naïveté were summed up by Steve Vasilakos, a sidewalk peanut vendor who had witnessed a similar drama outside the White House 24 years before, when the U.S. entered the First World War. "Just three months—we finish them," he said.

Inside the White House, the full Cabinet assembled at 8:40 p.m. for a meeting that Roosevelt described as the most serious session since Lincoln met with his Cabinet at the outbreak of the Civil War 80 years earlier. At half past nine, Congressional leaders of both political parties arrived—although Roosevelt deliberately left out Representative Hamilton Fish of New York, the ranking Republican on the House Foreign Affairs Committee, who prior to the Japanese attack on Pearl Harbor had vociferously accused the President of being a warmonger. To the Cabinet members and congressmen, the President announced his intention to convene a joint session of the Senate and House on the following day. His purpose was to request a declaration of war against Japan.

Outside the President's study, the grave procession of visitors was observed by Edward R. Murrow, the correspondent whose radio reports from bomb-ravaged London during the Battle of Britain had deeply stirred American listeners. Murrow and his wife had been invited to dinner with the Roosevelts that evening. His wife had phoned the White House in the afternoon to ask if they were still expected. "We all have to eat," said Mrs. Roosevelt. "Come anyway." The Murrows dined with Mrs. Roosevelt while the President was busy working on the speech he was to give before the joint session of Congress.

Mrs. Murrow went home at 11 o'clock, but her husband stayed on. It was after midnight when he finally was ushered into the President's study to share a tray of sandwiches and beer with F.D.R. By this time the dimensions of the disaster had become appallingly evident—not only Pearl Harbor but also American bases on Guam, Wake Island and the Philippines had been attacked—and Roose-

FIVE BROTHERS' TRAGIC SACRIFICE

Among the thousands of servicemen killed in the Japanese attack on Pearl Harbor was a sailor by the name of William Ball, from Fredericksburg, Iowa. What distinguished Ball from so many others who died on that day in 1941 was not any special act of heroism, but the tragic chain of events his death set in motion at home.

When Ball's boyhood buddies, the five Sullivan brothers from the nearby town of Waterloo, received word of his death, they marched out together to enlist in the Navy. The Sullivans, who wished to avenge their friend, insisted that they remain together, and the Navy granted their wish. On November 14, 1942, the cruiser the brothers were serving on, the U.S.S. *Juneau,* was hit and sunk in a battle off Guadalcanal in the Solomon Islands.

Almost two months went by before Mrs. Thomas Sullivan got the news, which arrived not by the usual telegram but by special envoy: all five of her sons were reported missing in action in the South Pacific and presumed dead. Not since Mrs. Lydia Bixby of Boston lost five sons in the Civil War in 1864 had any one American family suffered so many dead in the service of its country.

The Navy awarded posthumous Purple Hearts to the brothers, and christened a new destroyer U.S.S. *The Sullivans* in their honor. The family became a national symbol of heroic sacrifice, further enhanced by the act of the only remaining child, a girl, who enlisted in the Navy as a WAVE.

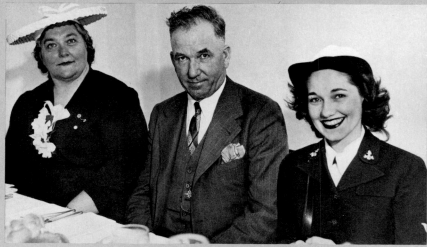

The Sullivan brothers—Joseph, Francis, Albert, Madison and George—stand, left to right, aboard the U.S.S. Juneau in 1942. Below is a picture of their parents, Mr. and Mrs. Thomas Sullivan, and their sister, Genevieve, in WAVE uniform, taken at a banquet in their honor at the premiere of a movie about the five.

velt was gray with exhaustion. Nonetheless, he appeared amazingly relaxed and eager to hear how the people of Britain were holding up. "I have seen certain statesmen of the world in time of crisis," Murrow later wrote. "Never have I seen one so calm and steady." Only once did the President's anger surface. In describing the bombing of Pearl Harbor, he told Murrow that 188 American planes had been destroyed on the ground—"on the ground, by God, on the ground!"

The President went before the joint session of Congress at 12:30 in the afternoon on December 8. The occasion was shared by a record radio audience of 60 million people across the nation. After hobbling in on the arm of his son James, who was dressed in the uniform of a Marine captain, he was introduced by the Speaker of the House, Sam Rayburn of Texas. Clutching the lectern with both hands, the President stood erect for the duration of his speech, in spite of the 10-pound steel braces that he wore on his legs. His voice was stern but confident.

"Yesterday, December 7, 1941—a date which will live in infamy," he said, "the United States of America was suddenly and deliberately attacked by naval and air forces of the empire of Japan." The President reported that many American lives had been lost at Pearl Harbor and that the Japanese had also attacked Malaya, Hong Kong, Guam, the Philippines, Wake and Midway. "Hostilities exist," he said. "I ask that the Congress declare that since the unprovoked and dastardly attack by Japan on Sunday, December 7, 1941, a state of war has existed between the United States and the Japanese Empire."

When he had completed his 10-minute speech, the Capitol fairly shook with applause, shouts and shrill whistles. In less than an hour, and with no debate, both houses approved the declaration of war against Japan. In the Senate the vote was 82-0. "The only thing now is to do our best to lick hell out of them," cried Senator Burton K. Wheeler, the former archisolationist from Montana. In the House, which had been so isolationist that four months earlier an extension of the draft had squeaked through by only one vote, there was only a single dissenter. She was Jeannette Rankin, a Republican from Montana and a pacifist who had voted against the United States' entry into the First World War in 1917. Now, after voting "nay," she was so shaken that she hid in a phone booth to escape reporters' questions.

At 4:10 p.m. Roosevelt signed the declaration of war. After 23 years and 25 days of peace, the U.S. was again at war. Three days later Japan's Axis partners, Germany and Italy, declared war on the United States, and Congress reciprocated in kind.

The most palpable consequence of the Japanese attack was the forging of an unprecedented degree of unity in the U.S. As columnist Arthur Krock wrote in *The New York Times*, "You could almost hear it click into place." On December 10, in fact, a public opinion poll found that only 2 per cent of Americans disapproved of the declaration of war against Japan. Moreover, Hitler's Nazi Germany seemed to virtually all Americans the embodiment of evil. John W. Flannagan Jr., a Democrat from Virginia, did not exaggerate his country's righteous wrath when he thundered on the floor of the House: "It is a war of purification in which the forces of Christian peace and freedom and justice and decency and morality are arrayed against the evil pagan forces of strife, injustice, treachery, immorality and slavery."

Pearl Harbor had ended years of confusion and uncertainty. The prewar years, the essayist E. B. White observed, "were like the time you put in in a doctor's waiting room, years of fumbling with old magazines and unconfirmed suspicions, the ante years, the time of the moist palm and the irresolution."

Those years had been marked by a series of adroit Roosevelt maneuvers that stopped just short of an outright declaration of war but that edged the nation ever closer to active participation on the Allies' side. In 1940 the President had secretly negotiated the trade of 50 overage destroyers to Great Britain in exchange for leases on six naval and air bases in the West Indies. The inception of America's first peacetime draft had been inaugurated in that same year, and then, early in 1941, Lend-Lease had made legal the transfer of war supplies to Britain and the Soviet Union. Most Americans supported these steps, but the country was still ambivalent about direct involvement of the U.S. A poll taken by *Fortune* magazine a few months before Pearl Harbor indicated that 70 per cent were opposed to entering the War but 67 per cent were ready to follow Roosevelt into it. In the midst of this confusion, said *Time* magazine, Pearl

Harbor had come "like a reverse earthquake that in one terrible jerk shook everything disjointed, distorted, askew back into place."

Some observers felt that the War would be a boon to the country, at least economically and in terms of morale. They pointed out that when America joined the fighting, the Depression-crippled economy still was sputtering along at a fraction of its potential speed. Four million Americans were unemployed, and 7.5 million others were earning less than the legal minimum wage of 40 cents per hour. In order to produce the needed tanks, ships, planes and guns, the economy would have to go all out, and every available worker would be needed. Moreover, many commentators suggested that the war effort would give the nation a new sense of direction and spiritual purpose after the self-indulgence of the Roaring Twenties and the near despair of the Depression Thirties. "We are alive, rudely awakened," wrote Jonathan Daniels, the young newspaper editor who later served as Roosevelt's assistant press secretary. "We are men again in America."

The new sense of unity and purpose was given added impetus when that majestic symbol of Great Britain's courage, Prime Minister Winston Churchill, arrived at the White House two weeks after the bombing of Pearl Harbor for a conference with Roosevelt. A grumpy, plump cherub whose eloquent voice already was familiar to American radio listeners, Churchill presented a striking visual contrast to his tall, jaunty host: Churchill with his horn-rimmed glasses and long black cigar; Roosevelt with his pince-nez and debonair cigarette holder.

The two heads of state had held their first meeting four months earlier, in mid-August, on ships anchored off the coast of Newfoundland. There they had drawn up the Atlantic Charter, a statement of their countries' postwar aims, and they had hit it off famously.

Churchill was a guest at the White House for three weeks after Pearl Harbor, turning the place upside down. Mrs. Roosevelt had arranged for him to sleep in the Lincoln bedroom, but he did not like the bed there so he tried out others until he found one that suited him: in the Rose Suite opposite the quarters occupied by his old friend Harry Hopkins, who handled Lend-Lease to Britain. Every morning

when Churchill awakened, he was served Scotch by a butler. The rest of the day he drank brandy. At night, wearing a siren suit that hugged his egg-shaped body, the Prime Minister wheeled the President about the blacked-out White House. One of their favorite haunts was Churchill's traveling map room, which was installed next to Hopkins' office for global strategy sessions.

On Christmas Eve, Churchill shared in the traditional tree-lighting ceremony on the South Portico and joined Roosevelt in broadcasting holiday greetings to his new American allies. The broadcast, and his subsequent address to a special joint session of Congress, gave Churchill particular pleasure because—as he often remarked—he had a certain "blood-right" to be in the United States. His mother was an American and one of her ancestors had been a lieutenant in George Washington's army. "The fact that my American forebears have for so many generations played their part in the life of the United States and that here I am, an Englishman, welcomed in your midst makes this experience one of the most moving and thrilling in my life, which is already long and has not been entirely uneventful," he told Congress. Then, peering over his glasses at the assembled legislators, the Prime Minister went on, "I cannot help reflecting that if my father had been American and my mother British, instead of the other way around, I might have got here on my own."

Churchill predicted—with sharp foresight—that the end of 1942 would see the Allies "quite definitely in a better position than we are now," and that 1943 "will enable us to assume the initiative upon an ample scale." He avowed his hope and faith that the two countries would "walk together in majesty, in justice and in peace." The tumultuous ovation that followed brought tears to his eyes, and when Churchill gave the two-fingered V-for-Victory sign that was his hallmark, U.S. Chief Justice Harlan Stone, seated opposite the dais, grinned and flashed back the sign.

Before the new year, Roosevelt and Churchill arrived at several major decisions. They would give first priority to the defeat of Germany, turning later to the task of finishing off Japan. They would combine their countries' resources, plan operations jointly and unite their forces into a single command. They framed a declaration expressing the determination of all Allied nations to use their full resources to defeat

A workman spreads a coat of dull gray paint over the gold-leaf dome of the Massachusetts State House on Beacon Hill in Boston nearly three months after Pearl Harbor. One of many precautions taken nationwide out of fear of aerial attack, the disguise was intended to make the State House a less conspicuous target for enemy bombardiers.

the Axis and pledging themselves not to make a separate peace with their enemies.

In the declaration, the Allied nations were referred to as the "Associated Powers," a name that did not satisfy either man. But on New Year's Eve, Roosevelt had an inspiration, and the following morning, while still in pajamas, he was wheeled to Churchill's room. Churchill was taking a bath and he answered Roosevelt's knock stark naked, pink and dripping "like a fat cherub," as Roosevelt told the story. Churchill himself quipped: "The Prime Minister of Great Britain has nothing to conceal from the President of the United States!"

Recalling their dissatisfaction with the title Associated Powers, the President said, "How about United Nations?"

"That should do it," replied Churchill, and he quoted a passage from Lord Byron's *Childe Harold,* where the term

occurred: *Here, where the sword united nations drew/Our countrymen were warring on that day!*

On New Year's Day, the Declaration of the United Nations was signed by the Big Four—Churchill, Roosevelt, the Soviet Ambassador and the Chinese Foreign Minister. The following day the Declaration was subscribed to by representatives of 22 other nations that were formally at war with the Axis. Thus the seeds of the United Nations organization were sown.

The initial euphoria of the War began to fade during the first months of the new year, 1942. Though the jukeboxes around the U.S. rasped out such jaunty tunes as "Goodbye, Mama, I'm Off to Yokohama" and "You're a Sap, Mister Jap," these were the darkest days of the War. U.S. and British forces were being routed in the Pacific: Guam fell,

then Manila, then Singapore, and—worst of all from an American point of view—Bataan and Corregidor.

Closer to home, along the Atlantic coast, the presence of German submarines was so menacing that when Churchill left for London in mid-January, he chose to make the journey by plane instead of by the British battleship that had brought him to the United States. The German U-boat fleet was riding high now. Submarines prowled unmolested up and down the east coast, from Canada to the Gulf of Mexico and the Caribbean, preying upon U.S.-bound tankers and freighters sailing for Britain with guns, tanks and planes. From January until the end of May, 87 ships were sunk in American waters.

In Manhattan, black paint was daubed over the gold-leaf roof of the Federal Building so it would not gleam in the moonlight and give enemy submarines an easy fix on the shore. But the neon glow of Miami and its suburbs provided an inviting six-mile backdrop for U-boat targets, and tourists on the beaches watched the burning ships go down offshore. Many of the one-sided battles occurred within sight of land. Survivors of the attacks staggered ashore, and debris and bodies from their ships littered the shores. Beaches were fenced off by the Navy to keep out the curious and to prevent people from learning the full dimensions of the U-boat debacle.

The fact was at this point that the U.S. was woefully incapable of defending itself. When President Roosevelt was asked by a reporter in February whether the U.S. was open to enemy attack, he gloomily replied, "Enemy ships could swoop in and shell New York; enemy planes could drop bombs on war plants in Detroit; enemy troops could attack Alaska."

"But," persisted the astonished reporter, "aren't the Army and Navy and the Air Force strong enough to deal with anything like that?"

"Certainly not," said the President.

As if to confirm his pessimism, a week later the War's first direct enemy attack on the continental U.S. occurred. At twilight on February 23, while Roosevelt was delivering one of his periodic radio reports to the nation, a lone Japanese submarine surfaced approximately one mile offshore north of Santa Barbara, California, and began lobbing shells at an oil refinery. Lawrence Wheeler, the proprietor of a nearby inn, was listening to Roosevelt on the radio when he heard the noise and went outside to investigate. "One of their shots whistled over my inn, which is a good mile from the shoreline," he recalled. "Their shooting wasn't very good." The sub fired 25 shells in 20 minutes, but only minor damage was done to the refinery.

Across the nation, as the magnitude of the Pearl Harbor devastation sank in, a virulent hatred of all things Japanese emerged. In Yonkers, New York, the owner of a curio shop took ax and hammer, smashed every item in his store that was marked "Made in Japan" and piled the pieces in his shop window. In Nashville, when the Tennessee Department of Conservation asked the purchasing department for six million licenses to hunt Japanese invaders at a fee of two dollars apiece, the answer came back: "Open season on 'Japs'—no license required." In Washington, D.C., along the Tidal Basin, hotheads chopped down four of the 3,000 Japanese cherry trees that had been presented to America by the citizens of Tokyo in 1912.

Suspicion and hatred encompassed all "enemy aliens" in the U.S., a category that included everyone of Japanese, German or Italian birth who lacked American citizenship. There were about 900,000 persons living in the U.S. who fit that description.

Prior to the Second World War, the concern was primarily for the German-Americans. The German-American Bund, a Nazi front group, had staged noisy rallies and sponsored the showing of propaganda films in German-American enclaves such as the Yorkville section of Manhattan and the German quarter of St. Louis. The Italian-Americans did not appear to be much of a threat. Many had taken pride in the accomplishments of Mussolini's Italy, and in the prewar days most of the Italian-American newspapers in the United States were pro-Fascist. But President Roosevelt probably reflected a widely held attitude when he told his Attorney General, "I don't care so much about the Italians, they are a lot of opera singers, but the Germans are different. They may be dangerous."

After war was declared, about 5,000 German-Americans and Italian-Americans were rounded up—including the opera singer Ezio Pinza, who was interned briefly at Ellis Island. Within a year most of the 5,000 were released. The hatred focused on the Japanese-Americans. Because of their race, they were highly visible, and people automatically equated them with the enemy pilots who had struck at Pearl Harbor and enemy troops who were now routing American forces in the Pacific. Of the 127,000 Japanese-Americans living in the U.S., about two thirds were native-born American citizens, but this did not allay the suspicions and hostility that were directed toward them.

Most of the Japanese-Americans lived in California, Oregon and Washington, where war jitters had been particularly acute ever since Pearl Harbor. With the Pacific Fleet crippled, residents on the West Coast felt they were vulnerable to a Japanese invasion at any moment. In this atmosphere, the anti-Oriental racism that had plagued the West Coast for nearly a century boiled over. The ugly mood was succinctly expressed by columnist Henry McLemore of the Hearst newspapers' anti-Oriental *San Francisco Examiner.* "Herd 'em up, pack 'em off," McLemore wrote. "Let 'em be pinched, hurt, hungry and dead up against it."

The hatred frequently erupted in violence and property damage, although the Japanese-Americans were not always without their defenders. Perhaps the most poignant drama occurred on skid row in Los Angeles where the folk singer Woody Guthrie had just blown into town with a side-kick named the Cisco Kid. Woody and Cisco were singing, for nickles and dimes and free drinks, to the sailors at the Ace High Bar when they heard glass crashing at the bar next door. Rushing outside, they found framed in the shattered glass window of the Imperial Bar the owner and his wife, who were both Japanese-Americans. On the far side of the street was a jeering mob. Guthrie and his partner, along with a few sailors and a woman who was carrying a gallon jug of wine, positioned themselves between the mob and its targets. Then Guthrie began to strum his guitar and sing the words of an old union song: "We will fight together/We shall not be moved." Passersby linked arms with the little group and took up the song. By the time the police arrived, the mob had faltered and shuffled away into the night.

As the pressure for action against the Japanese-Americans mounted, President Roosevelt on February 19, 1942, signed Executive Order 9066, authorizing the Secretary of War to prescribe certain "military areas" and to exile "any or all" persons from them. Though couched in broad language, the order was aimed at Japanese-Americans.

In the spring and summer of 1942, under this order, 112,000 Japanese-Americans were removed to temporary camps. Eventually they were shipped farther inland to 10 permanent camps in barren and isolated areas of six Western states and Arkansas *(pages 28-41).* Most of those forced to leave their homes were held in the camps for at least three years. Significantly, not a single Japanese-American was ever brought to trial on charges of espionage or sabotage—either in the United States or in Hawaii, where Japanese planes had shattered the peace of that December Sunday. The truth is that, in those turbulent four months after Pearl Harbor, too few Americans had the calm good sense to raise questions of the kind asked by the famous actor John Barrymore. One day in 1942, at the door of his California mansion, Barrymore saw his Japanese-American gardener Nishi with his family and their belongings waiting to be carried away by soldiers. Barrymore was dying, his mind fading in and out of reality, and he did not understand what was happening. When someone explained that America was at war with Japan, Barrymore could only murmur: "But is there a war on with Nishi and his family?"

BITTER EXILE IN THE U.S.

Wind billows the Stars and Stripes as a dust storm swirls around barracks at a desolate Japanese-American relocation camp in the desert at Manzanar, California.

AN EXODUS FORCED BY HATE AND FEAR

In February 1942, after President Roosevelt had signed an order authorizing the evacuation of Japanese-Americans from the West Coast, James Omura, a spokesman for the minority group, angrily asked a Congressional committee: "Has the Gestapo come to America?"

It must have appeared that way to 127,000 Japanese-Americans. Even though most of them were American citizens, a wave of prejudice and hatred engulfed them in the days that followed Pearl Harbor. Banks refused to cash their checks; insurance companies canceled their policies; milkmen and grocers refused to deliver or sell to them.

"A Jap's a Jap!" declared Lieut. General John L. DeWitt, charged with the West Coast's defense. "It makes no difference whether he's an American or not." Late in March, DeWitt's men began rounding up the Japanese-Americans for the evacuation. Many were given as little as 48 hours to dispose of their homes, businesses and farms; in the process they fell prey to bargain hunters who acquired their belongings for a fraction of their true value. Then, dragging baggage and bedrolls, and with their children tagged like pieces of luggage, these displaced Americans were carted off to assembly centers—hastily converted fairgrounds or race tracks, where many had to bed down in stalls still reeking of manure. Most went without protest, some stoic in their belief that compliance would certify their loyalty to the nation that was dishonoring them. Eventually they were shipped inland to isolated barracks cities—President Roosevelt himself once referred to them as concentration camps—where they lived as prisoners. After they had been in the camps about a year, their rights began to be restored and some were allowed to resettle in communities outside the West Coast area.

The young among them seemed to weather the confinement and readjust to freedom without lasting scars. But many of the elderly internees, weary and too old to start over, were reluctant to leave the comparative security of the camps. "Where shall we go?" one asked. "What shall we do at the twilight of the evening of our lives?"

A soldier on Bainbridge Island, Washington, hammers up placards notifying the Japanese-American residents of their impending evacuation.

To demonstrate his loyalty, a Japanese-American grocer displayed his nationality for everyone to see; as the topmost sign indicates, he still had to get out.

A Japanese-American woman solemnly pauses in the driveway of the stately home that she was forced to exchange for a single room in a flimsy barracks.

Clutching her pocketbook and a half-eaten apple, a bewildered child sits numbly amid her family's belongings as she awaits transport out of Los Angeles.

Facing a row of armed soldiers, evacuees from Los Angeles line up for inspection after arriving at an assembly center set up at the Santa Anita race track.

Three generations of a Japanese-American family gather at the stoop of a tiny dwelling place in the Salinas, California, assembly center, one of 15 crudely constructed camps on the West Coast where the evacuees were held until more permanent camps were built farther inland.

Exiles from the West Coast arrive by the truckload at their new home in the Wyoming desert, the Heart Mountain Relocation Center. In the camp, temperatures plunged to 30° below zero in winter, and the residents had to bank the earth against their barracks to keep out the icy winds.

A BARREN EXISTENCE IN MAKESHIFT CAMPS

"Every place we go we cannot escape the dust," wrote a Japanese-American youngster of his Topaz, Utah, internment camp. "Inside of our houses, in the laundry, in the latrines, in the mess halls, dust and more dust, dust everywhere." All except two of the 10 camps were situated in barren, desolate desert country. Each family was assigned to an "apartment"—one room measuring 20 by 25 feet—in a wooden barracks covered with tar paper.

"Aside from the absurdity of living that way," an internee later recalled, "life went on pretty much as usual." The Japanese-Americans maintained a stable small-town existence, complete with fire, police and post-office departments, schools, hospitals and camp-written newspapers. And even though they had been imprisoned by their own government, many began their days by pledging allegiance to the American flag. Furthermore, the Japanese-Americans were subject to the draft; 8,000 served in the U.S. armed forces, many with great distinction in combat overseas.

35

A Japanese-American woman and her children beat the heat and the monotonous routine of camp life by wading in the refreshing waters of a brook near the Manzanar Relocation Center in the California desert.

Costumed Japanese-Americans at the Tule Lake Relocation Center in northern California entertain their fellow internees by staging a production that they grandly called the Cabaret Internationale.

With their faces masked to prevent inhalation of harmful fibers, women internees aid the U.S. war effort by weaving camouflage netting. For this and other jobs, the U.S. paid the camp residents up to $19 a month.

A Japanese-American farmer from Auburn, Washington, who owned and operated his own poultry business for 10 years before being interned, gathers eggs in the camp henhouse at the Tule Lake Relocation Center.

The one-room apartment of the Hosokawa family, internees at the Heart Mountain Relocation Center, was a typical camp dwelling with Army-issue cots, a potbellied stove, and shelves and furniture made from scrap lumber. Pictures and curtains made the drab cubicle more livable.

Japanese-American soldiers on leave from the U.S. Army visit with their relatives in the USO center at the Heart Mountain internment camp. "The biggest irony of all," one young internee later recalled, "was seeing my three older brothers being drafted, one by one, out of our camp."

A Buddhist temple in Los Angeles lies ransacked during the wave of anti-Oriental feeling.

HANDIWORK OF VANDALS AND VIGILANTES

In the fall of 1942, the War Relocation Authority, which was created by the government to run the internment camps, began a campaign to channel the Japanese-Americans into communities outside the West Coast "war zone." Many towns were still seething with hatred for the Japanese. When five men who had been interned in one camp went to work for a New Jersey farmer, local vigilantes set fire to the farm. A Japanese-American girl who found a job in Denver was told by the minister of her new church that she might feel more at home in her own place of worship.

By the end of the war with Japan, however, some 55,000 Japanese-American internees had taken up life again outside the barbed wire. Those who eventually went back to their homes on the West Coast often found their property vandalized, their farms gone to seed and their businesses bankrupt. During their exile, the Japanese-Americans lost nearly half a billion dollars in assets—of which only about 10 per cent was returned by a repentant federal government two decades later.

An abandoned West Coast farmhouse is littered with leaves and trash; its Japanese-American owners were detained at one of the crowded internment camps.

2

In the wake of the Pearl Harbor attack, everyone seemed ready to join up. Practically everyone wanted to enlist in the war effort. Army and Navy recruiting stations and civilian-defense headquarters were deluged with volunteers. In Detroit, three generations of one family—grandfather, father and son—showed up at the Navy recruiting station. In Washington, D.C., the revered military leader of World War I, General of the Army John J. "Black Jack" Pershing, now 81 and infirm, was driven over to the White House from his suite at the Walter Reed Medical Center to offer his services. At Overbrook, Kansas, Edward Brentlinger got on his bicycle and rode 28 miles to Topeka to enlist. Hollywood film star Jimmy Stewart fattened up his spindly frame so he could make the minimum weight requirement for the Army Air Forces, and economics professor Paul Douglas of the University of Chicago joined the Marines as a buck private at age 50. Lyndon Johnson and Gerald Ford joined up. So did Joe DiMaggio, Gene Autry, Texas newspaper publisher Mrs. Oveta Culp Hobby and a high-school kid in a suburb of Philadelphia who wanted to be a fighter pilot and ate so many carrots to sharpen his vision that his skin briefly turned orange.

Volunteers and draftees, movie stars and farm kids, professors and students, center fielders and congressmen were joining up. To be of military age and not in uniform was to be physically or mentally impaired, or the subject of suspicion and innuendo about one's connections or courage. All told, nearly 16 million Americans wore a uniform during the War, about four times the number who served during World War I. At any given time late in the War, some 12 million were in the service, one in every 11 Americans. Able-bodied men in civilian clothes became so scarce that, in professional baseball, the St. Louis Browns resorted to using a one-armed outfielder named Pete Gray. A popular song lamented that the men who were left behind were "either too young or too old; they're either too bald or too bold." And in Hollywood, where most of the leading males were in uniform, an agent summed up for a producer his newest draft-proof discovery: "I've got a prospect for you —a young guy with a double hernia."

As the waves of newly inducted servicemen shuttled between training camps, shipped out for overseas, traveled home to wives and sweethearts or simply went out for a

AMERICA JOINS UP

night on the town, suddenly uniforms were everywhere. In the 16 days that followed Pearl Harbor, railroads on the home front moved more than 600,000 troops. Train stations and bus terminals became kaleidoscopes of olive drab, navy blue, marine green.

The uniforms, like many other things in military life, were known as Government Issue, or GI. And the swarms of men who wore them took for themselves the same unromantic label, GI. Though many GIs were volunteers, fully two thirds joined up through a system that was largely alien to America, conscription. Until 1940, the U.S. had been one of the few countries in the world that lacked a program of compulsory military training. Then, in September of that year, Congress approved the Selective Training and Service Act, the first peacetime draft in American history. Highly controversial, it was approved only after several weeks of sharp debate. Opposition from some quarters was extremely bitter. One clergyman predicted that the draft would reduce American youth to "syphilis and slavery."

The new law required all men between the ages of 21 and 35 to register with their local draft boards on the 16th of October. On that day, at 6,175 draft boards across the country, 16,316,908 men registered. The lines at local draft boards included executives and truck drivers, Fords and Rockefellers, factory workers and field hands. Their mood, reported *The New York Times,* "seemed to be philosophical resignation"—certainly not that of "a day of mourning for the death of the American way of life," as the registration was dubbed by the Socialist leader Norman Thomas.

Every man who registered received a draft number. Two weeks after the registration, President Roosevelt, Secretary of War Henry L. Stimson and other officials met in Washington around an enormous glass bowl to determine the order in which the registrants would be drafted. The bowl, which had been used for the same purpose in 1917 when the U.S. entered World War I, contained 9,000 bright blue capsules. In each capsule was a numbered slip of paper. The numbers, from 1 through 9,000, corresponded to the ones assigned registrants by their local draft boards.

When the moment for the plucking of the numbers from the glass bowl arrived, an aide blindfolded Secretary Stimson with a swatch of upholstery taken from a chair used 164 years before by the signers of the Declaration of Independence. Stimson then drew the first capsule from the bowl and handed it to the President, who extracted the slip of paper and read the number into a battery of radio microphones. The number was 158. "That's my son," shrieked a woman in the audience. Across the land there were 6,175 registrants with the same number. Among the holders of 158 was Alden C. Flagg Jr. of Boston. Twenty-three years earlier his father had held the first number plucked from the glass bowl by World War I Secretary of War Newton D. Baker. The fateful number then was 258.

Once the numbers had been picked, questionnaires were sent out by local draft boards to all registrants in the order of the selections from the bowl. Those who appeared from the answers to be qualified for service were then given a physical examination. After that the registrants were classified according to their fitness for the draft. Those who were fit were then called up in the order of the drawing of the numbers from the glass bowl. Those with number 158 who were qualified for military service would go first.

The decision as to who was fit was made by the all-powerful local draft board. The board was an eminently democratic group, consisting of three or more persons who were at least 36 years old and residents of the country over which they had jurisdiction—in short, the older friends and neighbors of the young men upon whom they might have to pass judgment. Volunteers who served without pay, they were appointed by the President upon recommendation of the state's governor. The boards ranged in manner of operation from the bureaucratic formality of the big city to the country folksiness of the one in Fentrees County, Tennessee, that was presided over by the famous Sergeant Alvin York. A World War I hero who had earned the Congressional Medal of Honor by killing 25 Germans and singlehandedly capturing 132 others, York had a special feeling for the problems of the young men under his jurisdiction. Before his own induction in 1917 he had at first refused to serve on religious grounds, insisting "War's agin the Book." Now, when a draftee filed an appeal, York and other board members would journey through the mountains to the man's home and conduct the hearing on his front porch.

The spirit of the draft was set by the director of Selective Service, Brigadier General Lewis B. Hershey, who favored local civilian control and wanted to keep red tape at a minimum. A square-framed professional soldier with a wiry brush of reddish-gray hair and the voice of a drill sergeant, Hershey would survive for three decades in an essentially thankless job. "Let's keep this thing so simple," he said, "that even crooks will say, 'I'll be patriotic and register just like all the other guys.' " Indeed, special draft boards were set up in most state and federal prisons, and more than 100,000 convicted felons were taken into the armed forces.

The local boards had a great deal of leeway in classifying a potential draftee. They could place him in any of more than a dozen different classifications, which ranged from 1-A ("available for military service") to 4-F ("physically, mentally or morally unfit for service").

Those who were classified 1-A soon found a form letter in their mailboxes. "Greeting," it began. "Having submitted yourself to a local board composed of your neighbors for the purpose of determining your availability for training and service in the armed forces of the United States, you are hereby notified that you have been selected for training and service in the Army." The letter, signed by a member of the local board, told the draftee when and where to report.

Deferment from the draft was based on a wide variety of reasons, including conscientious objection, economic de-

pendency of family or relatives and employment in an essential occupation such as farming. By 1944 almost two million farmworkers had been given occupational deferments on the ground that their employment was essential to the national defense. Nevertheless, even down on the farm there were some exceptions. A 70-year-old man who operated a 765-acre farm in Illinois with the help of his six grown sons lost five of them to the draft. And the sixth son would have been inducted if he had not suffered a broken hip in an accident.

Marriage alone did not warrant deferment, though many young men assumed it would, and one of the nation's largest manufacturers of wedding rings, J. R. Woods & Sons, reported a 250 per cent increase in sales after the Selective Service Act was approved.

In the first years of the draft, fathers were excused from military service. Babies were called "draft insurance," and by mid-1943, eight million fathers were deferred. But as the manpower pool dwindled and demands from the battlefronts increased, more and more fathers lost their deferments. The change in status was opposed in Congress, where one Senator insisted that "slackers in the government bureaus" ought to be inducted "before American homes

are broken up." But by the end of 1944, only 80,000 men still held deferments as fathers.

The burgeoning manpower needs forced Selective Service to conduct a total of eight different registrations. The age span was broadened to include all men from 18 through 65, though only those between 18 and 36 were actually called up. In the fourth registration, on April 27, 1942, the 60-year-old President of the United States registered and received the draft card that he kept in his wallet until he died.

In view of the enormous number of registrants—nearly 50 million—there were remarkably few attempts to evade the draft. Most of the 348,217 cases logged by Selective Service involved technical violations, such as filling out a form incorrectly, rather than outright evasion. Some men attempted to avoid service by faking deafness, heart ailments or mental disorders. However, the prize for attempted draft evasion belonged to Everett Stewart of Valley Station, Kentucky. Stewart kept the local board posted on the alleged deterioration of his health by impersonating various of his concerned loved ones—a sister, half brother, father and crippled old uncle. Finally, wearing a wig and floppy hat, he appeared at the board as the bereaved widow to report his own death. For his performance, Stewart was sentenced to three years in the federal penitentiary at Atlanta.

Rejections for legitimate reasons, however, were the most frustrating problem faced by Selective Service during the War. An astonishing number of men—more than five million—were rejected for physical, educational or mental deficiencies. Until 1943 the Army was the only branch to rely on draftees, and it deliberately set its physical requirements at rock bottom. The minimum height for draftees was five feet and the minimum weight 105 pounds. The selectees had to have correctable vision and at least half of their natural teeth; they must not have flat feet, hernia or venereal disease. In 1941 the rejection rate was so high, about 50 per cent, that Franklin Roosevelt convened a national conference to investigate. The conference concluded that the chief causes of the rejections—bad teeth and bad eyes—could be traced to the shortage of basic medical care and the lack of adequate nutrition during the recent Depression.

Another major cause of rejection, illiteracy, could also be traced to the Depression and its crippling impact on public education. In the two draft registrations held before Pearl Harbor, 347,038 men out of a total of over 17 million had to sign their forms with a mark because they could not write their own names. Before the War was over, the Army needed men so desperately that it had to lift the ban on illiterates and set up special schools to try to bring the uneducated up to the fourth-grade level in reading. An Army teacher, Roger B. Goodman, wrote his parents of the learning agonies suffered by his GI students: "One boy, who was trying to read for me, started trembling and sweating. His hands, clutched around his pencil, were shaking like leaves and the sweat was standing out under the hair on his knuckles. A big drop of moisture rolled down his chin and plopped on the page. The soldier was so embarrassed that he put his fist over the stain so that I might not notice it."

The third major cause of rejection, emotional instability, accounted for the 4-F status of some three million men. The reasons for the high rate of rejections on this score are extremely complex and have never been completely untangled. The anxious times in which these men were living no doubt had something to do with the rejections, and there were other factors. The author Philip Wylie blamed what he called "Momism"—overprotective mothers. He may well have been right, in part at least. His view was supported by Dr. Edward Strecker, a psychiatric consultant to the Secretary of War, who said many women "had failed in the elementary mother function of weaning offspring emotionally as well as physically." Even those who were accepted often suffered from Momism, according to Wiley. In *Generation of Vipers* he wrote: "I cannot think, offhand, of any civilization except ours in which an entire division of living men has been used during wartime, or at any other time, to spell out the word 'mom' on a drill field."

Most Americans who were physically and mentally qualified were ready enough to take up arms for their country, but a small percentage chose not to serve for reasons of conscience. Of the 10,022,367 men ordered to report for induction, 42,973 were officially classified under the Selective Service Act as conscientious objectors "by reason of religious training and belief." Some 25,000 of the COs agreed to enter the service as medics or in other lines of duty that would not require them to bear arms. About 12,000 others worked at alternative nonmilitary service in

Typifying the plight of the Army enlisted man, cartoonist Sergeant George Baker's Sad Sack—a favorite of GI readers of Yank during World War II —loses out, even in his off-duty hours. Intent on a big time in town, he discovers—as many a private did—that the choicest spots are off limits, except to officers. When Baker's hero finally finds acceptance, the "Enlisted Men Only" notice lures him to a crowning ignominy.

151 Civilian Public Service Camps. The remaining 6,000 refused to serve in any capacity and were sent to federal prison. Most were Jehovah's Witnesses, Quakers, Mennonites or members of the Church of the Brethren. When a surprisingly large number of his coreligionists decided to accept induction after Pearl Harbor, one imprisoned war resister bitterly suggested that the prewar pacifists who changed their minds and went to war should be prosecuted.

Conscientious objectors with a clear-cut religious opposition to war were treated with more sympathy by draft boards and by the general public than those who balked at conscription on political or philosophical grounds. The War's most publicized CO, actor Lew Ayres, was a philosophical pacifist, whose belief stemmed in part from his celebrated role as a disillusioned German soldier in the film *All Quiet on the Western Front*. After Ayres was assigned to duty as a woodsman in a Civilian Public Service Camp, the public reaction to him was so adverse that many theaters refused to show films in which he was featured. One film starring Ayres, *Born to Be Bad,* was reshot by the producers with a new male lead. Later, Ayres distinguished himself with the Chaplains' Corps, caring for the dying and wounded under fire, on the island of Leyte in the Philippines.

Many of the COs in Civilian Public Service Camps were college-educated, highly trained professionals: teachers, social workers and artists. Some of them worked in mental hospitals, and about 500 volunteered to be infested with typhus-bearing lice or infected with malaria to test new serums. But most were assigned to menial labor—cutting trees and building roads—that neither suited their talents nor satisfied their intense personal desire to be socially useful. A Stanford University research chemist, Dr. Don DeVault, was assigned to digging ditches. In his spare time he did research on penicillin molds until he was sent to a special camp for "rebellious" objectors. He begged Selective Service to allow him to complete his penicillin studies but was ordered to report for further ditchdigging. When he refused, announcing he would work full time in his laboratory, he was prosecuted and imprisoned.

The COs in the camps, who worked without wages and paid for their own food and clothing, resented the military regimentation of the camps. In some instances their frustration boiled over into strikes and other passive resistance tactics borrowed from Mohandas K. Gandhi's independence movement in India.

In federal prisons, where COs accounted for every sixth inmate, COs staged work stoppages and hunger strikes to protest racial segregation, mail censorship and parole restrictions. At the Danbury Correctional Institution in Connecticut, 18 protestors went on strike for 135 days and won

a major victory when officials agreed to racially integrate the dining halls. The tactics were so effective that some of the same COs later used them in the civil-rights movement. Prison officials, accustomed to dealing with hardened criminals, had never seen anything like it. The superintendent of a Western prison said he yearned "for the good old days of simple murderers and bank robbers."

Even murderers and bank robbers found it hard to understand the COs. One CO tried to explain to the notorious Louis Lepke what had brought him to Danbury. At first Lepke, the boss of Murder, Inc., could not comprehend exactly what crime the CO had committed. Then suddenly he understood and asked incredulously, "You mean they put you in here for *not* killing?"

Most young men did not balk at entering the military service, however. If they were physically and mentally qualified, they were classified 1-A and given 10 days to tidy up their affairs. Then, on the appointed day, they gathered with 100 or so others at the designated point of departure—each one with a suitcase or bundle and often with his wife, girl friend or parents in tow.

In small towns, the going-away was a major local event. A typical send-off given to a group of recruits was described by the sociologist W. Lloyd Warner in his study of a town in Illinois, *Democracy in Jonesville*: "At 6:30 a crowd of people gathered outside a local cafe where the selectees were having their breakfast and receiving final instructions. Outside, the high school band would fall into position and next a color guard from the American Legion. As the boys came out of the door of the cafe, they lined up and the head of the draft board called 'Forward march.' They marched down Liberty Street to the railroad station where a large crowd had gathered. Everywhere little groups of people surrounded individuals about to leave. As the train would come around the curve from the west the conversation would pick up tensely and the band begin to play. Hurried kisses, embraces, and handshakes from relatives and friends. One by one the boys shook hands with the draft board and climbed onto the train. The train pulled out and the buzz of excitement in the crowd was drowned out by the band playing the Marine Hymn. Within a minute or two the station became deserted except for the two men loading mail and baggage onto a truck. Jonesville had made another contribution to the war."

The destinations of the trains and buses were stateside camps with such names as Dix, Benning and Meade. The arrival at one of these outposts was like stepping down on another planet. The climate, the culture and almost everything that moved could seem initially hostile to the newcomer. The boy from the North sweltered in the heat of Fort Benning, Georgia; the Southern boy shivered in the cold that blew across the drill fields at the Great Lakes Naval Training Center. At Camp McCoy, Wisconsin, one Brooklynite came back to his barracks bearing a set of rattles from a rattlesnake, explaining that he "got 'em off a big woim."

Inside the camp, the recruit found himself in an alien world of inch-long doctor's needles and half-inch crewcuts, of fat supply sergeants who doled out drab uniforms that did not always fit, growling "Buddy, this ain't Hart, Shaffner, or Marx!" The sharp break from civilian life was summed up in the story of the sergeant who was trying to quiet a group of draftees so he could swear them into the Army. "Gentlemen, please be quiet," he begged. Then, after they had taken the oath and were his to command, he roared, "Now, goddam it, SHUT UP!"

In training camp, the recruit gave up his civilian identity for a rank and serial number and surrendered his mind and body to a series of numbing rituals—morning calisthenics, marching in cadence of 128 steps per minute, practicing the manual of arms and performing the drudgeries of kitchen police. He learned a new vocabulary: "chow" for food; "on the double" for hurrying; "SNAFU" for "situation normal—all fouled up"; and "SOS" as the acronym for the chipped-beef-and-gravy abomination that was served to him on toast at six in the morning. (The "O" and "S" stood for ". . . on a shingle.")

The college graduates often had a particularly difficult time adjusting to barracks life. Many of them went into officers' training, but those who remained in the enlisted ranks found themselves in an environment that bore no resemblance to the college campus. They had to get used to country music and barracks language. They grumbled at the lack of decent reading matter, and the officers in one camp forbade them to read anything but the Bible during the first six weeks of training. When one recruit had his first chance

After registering for the draft in 1942, World War I hero Sergeant Alvin C. York (in hat and tie), stops to chat outside the same country store in Pall Mall, Tennessee, where he had been inducted 25 years earlier. The 54-year-old veteran was one of 13 million men between 45 and 64 who signed up in the country's fourth draft registration. Though York was raring to go, no one over 36 was actually called up; instead he served through the War as head of the draft board in Fentress County, Tennessee.

A TEXAS-SIZED RESPONSE TO A JAPANESE TRIUMPH

Shortly after midnight on March 1, 1942, the flagship of the U.S. Asiatic Fleet, the cruiser *Houston,* was sunk by the Japanese off the south coast of Java. The entire crew of 1,087 was either killed or captured.

Aroused by the sinking of their city's namesake, the citizens of Houston, Texas, vowed that they would get even. With the motto "Avenge the Houston!" as his talisman, district Navy public relations officer Clarence C. Taylor initiated a whirlwind campaign to recruit 1,000 men from the Houston area to replace the lost crewmen. A special enlistment station was set up, and an 80-foot replica of the *Houston* was built to attract recruits. Taylor's campaign was so successful that by Memorial Day, when the official swearing-in of the Houston volunteers was to take place, more than 1,400 men had enlisted.

In Navy uniform, Clarence C. Taylor awaits recruits.

Thousands jam Houston on May 30, 1942, to watch the swearing-in of Navy recruits whose local—and national—patriotism led them to join up.

48

to get off the base and go into town, he was surprised to find that he hungered for books more than for women; instead of going to town, he hurried to the camp library (where he was approached by a young sailor who asked, "Hey buddy, which is true—fiction or nonfiction?").

The noncommissioned officers who presided over the training of the fledgling soldiers and sailors—sergeants in the Army and Marines, petty officers in the Navy—were monsters unlike anything the recruits had ever seen. To the recruits it often seemed that the only object of these drill-masters was to make life miserable. "I shall nourish an all-encompassing hatred for him so long as I live," the newspaper reporter Jim Lucas wrote of a sergeant at his Marine boot camp. "He roared at us from the moment we appeared until the moment we left. Our bare existence, for which we were humbly apologetic, plagued him, and sent him into spasms of rage."

At times the treatment handed out by the sergeants and the officers was brutal. Dr. William C. Menninger, who was chief consultant in neuropsychiatry to the Army Surgeon General, recalled a medical officer who related to him "how well he had handled psychiatric problems when he was company commander." The officer had used a sergeant, a former boxer, to handle complaints from enlisted men by roughing them up. If the enlisted man came to the officer to report the beating, the officer would proudly point to the notice on the company bulletin board forbidding noncommissioned officers to even touch soldiers under their command. Surely the sergeant would not disobey orders, said the officer—perhaps the recruit had gotten his black eye in a collision with a door.

In the field, the recruit was exposed to a different kind of danger as he learned to dodge bullets in simulated combat, and to hug the ground and move forward while artillery fire whizzed overhead. "I've just had my first taste of advancing under fire," Corporal Melvin Fauer wrote to a friend from Camp Hood, Texas. "I'll admit I was scared sweatless, but now that it's over I know what Roosevelt meant when he said that we had nothing to fear but fear itself."

In the days before the American war machine began to run at its top speed, the recruits frequently trained with make-believe guns and tanks. They had to make do with painted wooden rifles, "machine guns" carved from two-by-four timbers and Ford trucks hung with placards proclaiming them to be tanks.

Resourceful commanders sometimes found strange ways to overcome the equipment shortages. In the Louisiana maneuvers in the summer of 1941, a tough but canny major general named George S. Patton Jr. was in command of an ill-equipped armored division. The division's tanks included an early 12-ton model that lacked a periscope, which meant that the tank commander had to ride with his head poking up through the turret—exposed to dust and mock fire—and deliver instructions to the driver through his feet: a kick in the back meant go forward; a kick in the right shoulder meant turn right. Some of Patton's tanks were so old that they were continually breaking down. When a mechanic told him the Army did not have the badly needed spare parts, but they could be ordered by mail from Sears, Roebuck, Patton sent off a mail order and paid for the parts out of his own pocket.

America's citizen-soldiers, like their ancestors in the Civil War and the Revolution, were a brash and unruly lot. They chafed under regimentation and lived for the day when they could chuck the military life and go home. In the months before Pearl Harbor, the recruits began chalking the word "OHIO"—for "over the hill in October"—on barracks walls, tanks and trucks, a threat that they might desert in the month when the draft law was due to expire.

To the dismay of some of their more hidebound commanders, the citizen-soldiers frequently showed almost no respect for rank. Their brashness surfaced in the Tennessee maneuvers of 1941 in one of the most celebrated and controversial home-front incidents of the War. On a hot midsummer afternoon, a truck convoy bearing 350 troops returning from a month in the field passed the Memphis Country Club. When the troops saw a group of girls in shorts strolling near the first tee, they set up a chorus of wolf whistles and shouts—"Yoo-hoo-o-o-o!" A soldier also yelled at the golfer on the first tee, "Fore!" When the golfer missed the ball entirely someone shouted, "Hey, buddy, do you need a caddy?"

With that, the golfer threw down his club, vaulted a three-foot fence and presented himself to the convoy. He was Lieut. General Ben Lear, commanding general of the

WOMEN WHO HEEDED THE CALL TO ARMS IN THE NATION'S HOUR OF NEED

To help recruit female college students, Eleanor Roosevelt (center) visited U.S. campuses with military directors (left to right) Mildred McAfee of the WAVES, Oveta Culp Hobby of the WACs, Ruth C. Streeter of the women Marines and Dorothy C. Stratton of the SPARs.

A WAVE takes aim with a pistol during target practice. Although women in the Navy were never assigned to combat duty, and few of them ever got to leave the United States, WAVES served as gunnery instructors for men.

At a time when almost every able-bodied man was away in uniform, women came out of the home to work in factories and foundries *(pages 88-101),* and to assume military roles hitherto performed by men.

The nationwide rush to enlist in the new Women's Army Auxiliary Corps startled recruiters *(pages 66-75).* Soon the other services as well opened their ranks to women, though there were many restrictions. The Navy took some 77,000 into the Women's Naval Reserve, but although WACs were allowed to serve overseas, it was not until late in 1944 that WAVES—Women Accepted for Volunteer Emergency Service—got to travel to such safe areas as Hawaii, Alaska and the Caribbean. Similar restrictions applied to the smaller groups of women Marines and the Coast Guard's SPARs— a contraction of *semper paratus,* Latin for "always ready."

The Army Air Forces—as the air force was then known—was so hesitant about enlisting women that it created an Army-supervised branch of the Civil Service, the Women's Auxiliary Ferrying Squadron. Female fliers, known as WAFS, underwent a stepped-up version of the pilots' training program, sometimes putting in 16-hour days drilling, mastering Morse code and map-reading, and flying single- and twin-engine planes. As pilots, they proved faster with instruments and smoother at the controls than their male counterparts. Nevertheless, WAFS were restricted to ferrying planes from factories to Army air bases.

The Navy made sure that the women under its command spent most of their time on land, operating control towers, repairing and maintaining everything from plumbing to parachutes, and performing whatever other tasks would free the men for combat duty.

By 1945, the number of women serving in the military was still small, but given society's preconceptions about the female role, as well as a fear of creating "new Amazons," the more than 200,000 women on active duty in the armed forces represented a breakthrough.

A pilot in training for the WAFS makes a solo flight in a single-engine plane. Officially members of the Civil Service rather than the Army Air Forces, WAFS nevertheless were trained by the Army and flew Army planes.

A female Marine operates a camera that was used for air reconnaissance. Women filled many ground positions at Marine air stations, directing air traffic and repairing aircraft engines as well as driving service vehicles.

Second Army during the maneuvers from which the troops were returning. After Lear chewed them out properly, he prescribed the punishment: a 300-mile round trip by truck to their quarters in Arkansas and back to Memphis, where they would pitch camp at the airport, then march 15 miles of the way back to Arkansas with full field gear. The troops took it in stride, singing an improvisation of the old World War I song as they marched, "Old Ben Lear, he missed his putt, parley voo. . . ." But throughout the rest of the maneuvers, civilians would line the streets and shout at the truck convoys, "Yoo-hoo-o-o-o!" There were loud protests about Lear's harsh discipline from parents and congressmen, but Franklin Roosevelt refrained from intervening.

For all its growing pains, the Army emerged from its mock battles and training routines as a modern fighting force. By Pearl Harbor, in less than two years, it had grown from 300,000 men—and what Chief of Staff General George Marshall described as "the status of that of a third-rate power"—to 1.5 million men organized into 31 combat divisions. Moreover, the organizational base for the wartime mobilization of eight million men was firmly set.

Even more important, perhaps, the maneuvers and the war games had brought to the forefront the men who would lead the nation's fighting forces throughout World War II: men like Patton and that inconspicuous newcomer Dwight D. Eisenhower. As Chief of Staff of the Third Army in the maneuvers of 1941, Colonel Eisenhower had conceived and directed the brilliant strategy that had routed the Second Army under "Yoo-hoo Ben Lear." Within the space of three years, Eisenhower would command the great invasion of Western Europe, but at the beginning of the War, he was so little known to the American public that a newspaper picture caption identified him as "Lt. Col. D. D. Ersenbeing." When Ike saw the photograph, he quipped, "At least the initials were right."

The War swept aside many strongly held prejudices toward servicemen. In the pre-Pearl Harbor days, men in uniform often were treated shabbily by the public. "Soldiers and dogs—keep out," read a sign in a restaurant near a training camp. But after America entered the War, servicemen were respected, and the uniform became a symbol of pride. Girls flocked to the soldiers, sailors and Marines. The marriage rate soared. In the first five months after Pearl Harbor an estimated 1,000 women a day married servicemen. In 1940 the motivation for many marriages had been the hope of avoiding the draft. Now, for many, it was the search for an emotional anchor among the new uncertainties of war. "I don't love him," a young woman told a sociologist. "I've told him I don't love him. But he's an aviator and he says I should marry him anyhow and give him a little happiness. He says he knows he'll be dead in a year."

The old taboos of class, family consent and lengthy courtship were swept aside. Quick courtships were the order of the day, and perhaps the most impressive was that of the movie star Private Mickey Rooney. Assigned to Camp Siebert, Alabama, he met a lovely 17-year-old who had just been named Miss Birmingham. He proposed to her on their first date and they were married after an engagement of only seven days. "I married Betty Jane because I was determined to marry someone," Rooney later wrote in his autobiography. "I'd had some drinks, was hurt and lonely, reached and grabbed."

Some of the quickie marriages involved unscrupulous young women, known as "Allotment Annies." After marrying, they received the $50 monthly allotment check due each serviceman's wife and were the beneficiaries of the GI's $10,000 life-insurance policy. Some married more than one GI at a time. One Allotment Annie specialized in combat pilots, who were known to have a high mortality rate. Another woman, who was only 17, worked as a hostess in a nightclub and specialized in sailors who shipped out from the big Naval base at Norfolk, Virginia. Two of her husbands met by chance in a pub in England and compared pictures of their wives. After the Shore Patrol broke up the fight, the two sailors joined forces to end the career of this particular Annie.

For most servicemen, courtship and marriage had to be carried on at long distance. At Camp Roberts, California, Private Wayne Harris spent an entire month's pay—$21 when the draft started, scarcely more than the $16 that Civil War recruits got 75 years before—on one long-distance call to his sweetheart in Los Angeles.

Some wives attempted to keep up with their husbands in the service. Disheveled and careworn, carrying babies, they crowded the bus and train stations, moving from one train-

ARCHITECTS OF WAR: THE TOP U.S. BRASS

Army Chief of Staff George C. Marshall (second from left) confers with other Joint Chiefs (left to right) Ernest J. King, William D. Leahy and Henry H. Arnold.

Although America's military leaders on the battlefields abroad garnered most of the home-front headlines, four men in Washington, D.C., the Joint Chiefs of Staff, were charged with deciding how the nation's military could most effectively combat the Axis enemy. Theirs was a chilling responsibility—to carve out a worldwide strategy for 11.2 million soldiers and airmen, 4.1 million sailors and more than half a million Marines.

The men who ran America's war effort from the home front were strikingly different. General George C. Marshall was known for his force of character and quiet dignity. Admiral Ernest J. King was just the opposite—outspoken, blunt and proud of his reputation for toughness. Lieut. General Henry H. Arnold, head of the U.S. Army Air Forces, earned himself the nickname "Hap" because of his genial manner. Admiral William D. Leahy, President Roo-

sevelt's brilliant and versatile Chief of Staff, was a skilled organizer.

All four bore heavy burdens, but the most important man was Marshall. So incisive was his mind and so respected was his judgment that when his name came up for the role of commander in the crucial invasion of Western Europe, President Roosevelt decided he was too valuable in Washington to be spared, and General Dwight D. Eisenhower was chosen instead.

ing camp to another. Near each camp, they set up house-keeping as best they could, often paying outrageous rents, cooking on Sterno stoves and seeing their mates for only a few hours at a time.

At Leesville, Louisiana, near Camp Polk, a reporter discovered young servicemen's wives paying up to $50 a month to live in sheds, converted chicken coops and ramshackle barns, which had been broken up into cubicles with make-shift partitions. In one place, a single toilet and shower served 35 families. The local milk apparently was unsafe, and several babies died. In Brunswick, Maine, a college town, the families of sailors at the nearby Naval air station were more fortunate. Many of them were taken into the homes of Bowdoin faculty members; one professor provided meals and lodging for 26 people.

For the servicemen who had nowhere else to go for enter-tainment, there was always the tawdry allure of the honky-tonk districts that sprang up around almost every training camp. Bearing such names as "The Strip" or "Bug Town," they were garish clusters of bars, dance halls, sleazy hotels or brothels. At Albany, Georgia, near Turner Field, the women in a brothel brazenly displayed their names in neon lights. Phoenix City, Alabama, across the Chattahoochee River from Fort Benning, Georgia, became so notorious for its brothels and brawls that it was known as Sin City.

Clergymen and other guardians of the public morality waged an unceasing war against the fleshpots. One unex-pected champion of continence was Lieut. Commander Gene Tunney, chief of the physical-fitness program for the Navy, who also happened to be a director of the American Distillers Corporation. In a *Reader's Digest* article entitled "The Bright Shield of Continence" the former heavyweight boxing champion of the world asserted that abstinence from sex kept men "at the peak of physical force." He urged all servicemen to remain chaste for the duration and insist-ed that "Any man above the emotional level of a tomcat must realize that the professional's embrace is not only a menace to health but a shameful desecration of ideal love."

The chief weapon of the reformers was the so-called May Act of 1941, which enabled local communities to shut down brothels near military installations. By 1944, some 700 mu-nicipalities had closed their red-light districts.

But shutting down organized prostitution only increased the vast army of streetwalkers and camp followers who operated near the military installations. The clampdown also was accompanied by a sharp increase in venereal dis-ease. Coupled with the desire to protect "nice girls" from predatory GIs, this led some spokesmen to advocate the establishment of special, supervised brothels for soldiers. "What substitute do we offer for prostitution?" asked a Navy surgeon, who then answered ominously, "Like it or not, somebody's daughter."

Most communities tried to provide alternatives to broth-els and red-light districts. Across the country, there were 3,000 USO—United Service Organization—centers where a GI could enjoy a clublike atmosphere and find a date for the Saturday-night dance. There were also hundreds of canteens sponsored by churches and local civic groups and occasional invitations for dinner or the weekend with private families. Famous personalities contributed their time to these servicemen's centers. At the New York Stage Door Canteen, the popular comedian Jack Benny served beer to GIs. At a canteen in the National Press Club in Washing-ton, D.C., GIs were entertained by Vice President Harry Tru-man's plunking out a waltz while film actress Lauren Bacall perched seductively atop the piano. Still, there was no substitute for the girl back home.

All of the problems of being in the service and away from home—the loneliness, the separation from loved ones and the shock of being wrenched from civilian ways—were intensified for some members of the armed services by sexual and racial discrimination. There were 300,000 wom-en in the service, the first representatives of their sex in the armed forces. The Army, Navy Air Corps, Marines and Coast Guard all had separate branches for women. They ferried planes, drove trucks, served as clerks and otherwise released men for combat duty.

The women in uniform were regarded as second-class citizen-soldiers. They had to endure the wisecracks of their fellow GIs and the derision of civilians who alternately accused them of lesbianism and heterosexual promiscuity and who feared they would get, in the military acronym, PWOP—"pregnant without permission." "Why can't these gals just stay home and be their own sweet self, instead of being patriotic," wrote a soldier trying to dissuade his sister from enlisting. A Marine officer put it more crudely, "Goddam it all," he told his first female arrivals. "First they send us dogs. Now it's women."

But the prejudice encountered by women was mild compared with that encountered by blacks. The 961,000 who entered the service faced a caste system far more rigid than the discrimination they had experienced in civilian life. For much of the War, a policy of strict racial segregation prevailed. In the training camps, blacks were relegated to separate eating and recreational facilities. Army units were segregated by race from the battalion to the division level and, in any unit, no black officer could outrank a white one.

At the beginning of the War, the Navy accepted blacks only as mess attendants; the Marines would not accept them at all. Intermingling of the races, said the official government policy—approved by President Roosevelt in 1940—"would produce situations destructive to morale and detrimental to the preparation for national defense." Furthermore, the Army, with the support of the American Red Cross, went so far as to segregate the blood plasma donated by blacks and whites, even though the man who had perfected the method for preserving plasma, Dr. Charles R. Drew, was himself black.

Secretary of War Stimson and many of his generals frankly believed that blacks were intellectually inferior—a belief reinforced by their generally poor performance on the Army General Classification Test. Products of a largely segregated and poorly funded educational system, most blacks scored in the bottom 40 per cent on the test. Psychologists have tended since then to conclude that the tests were biased in favor of middle-class whites and that the scores compiled by the blacks were depressed by inferior educational environments.

The experience of Jackie Robinson showed how pervasive racial prejudice was in the Army. Californian Robinson faced rigid discrimination for the first time in his life during his Army service. A lieutenant, he had the unenviable job of serving as a morale officer for a black company at Fort Riley, Kansas. One day, Robinson heard one of his men sum up the state of company morale: "They want to send me 10,000 miles away to fight for democracy when a hundred feet away they've got stools I can't put my black butt on and drink a bottle of beer."

The next day, Robinson telephoned the camp provost marshal to protest the segregated seating at the post exchange. "Nobody's going to separate any bullets and label them 'for white troops' and 'for colored troops,' " Robinson told him angrily. "Let me put it this way," said the provost, who was unaware his caller was black, "How would you like to have your wife sitting next to a nigger?"

Later, at Camp Hood, Texas, Robinson was court martialed after he refused to sit in the back of a bus on the post. Charges were filed against him and, though he was a teetotaler, he was given a test for drunkenness. When two major black newspapers got hold of the story, most of the charges were dropped and Robinson quickly was found not guilty of the remaining two charges.

Other blacks from the North ran afoul of Army prejudice and civilian hostility. The training camps were located largely in the South, and there were frequent outbreaks of violence. In 1941, black soldiers at Fayetteville, North Carolina, fought an hour-long gun battle with a company of white military police, leaving two men dead and five wounded. One of these clashes claimed the life of the first man ever killed with the Army's new basic infantry weapon, the M-1 rifle: he was a black American sergeant.

SHRUNKEN SHORTS FROM THE LAUNDRY

PREYED ON BY WOLVES IN SERGEANT'S CLOTHING

BOWLED OVER BY A RIFLE'S RECOIL

CUT DOWN TO SIZE BY THE FIRST SERGEANT

YOU'RE IN THE ARMY NOW

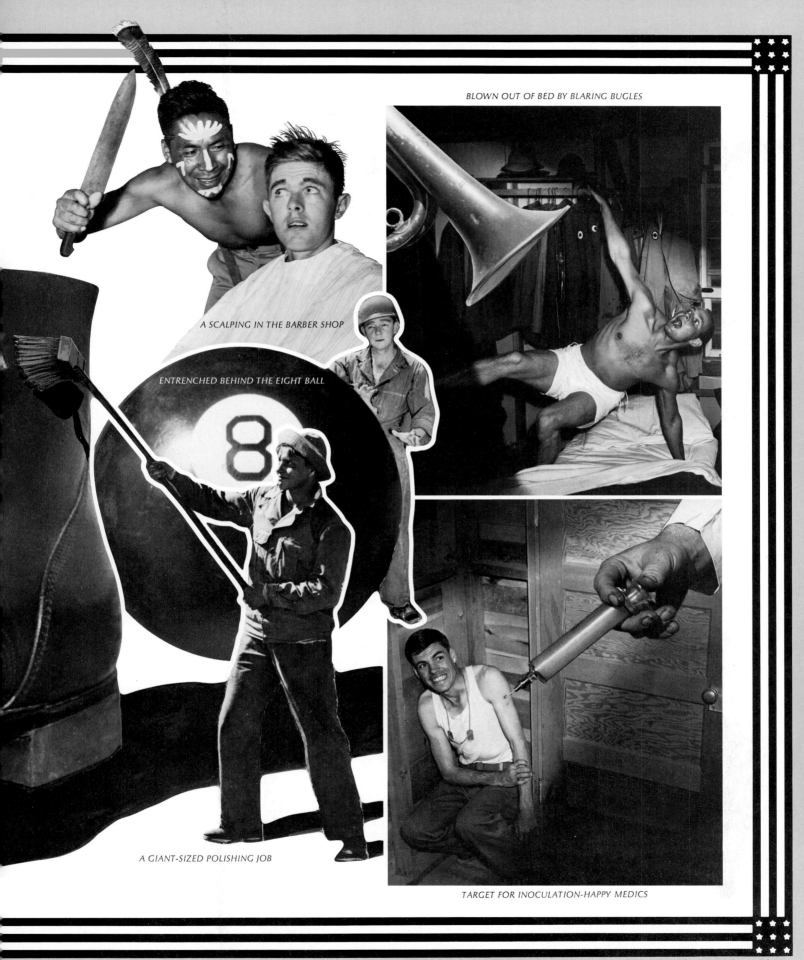

A SCALPING IN THE BARBER SHOP

ENTRENCHED BEHIND THE EIGHT BALL

A GIANT-SIZED POLISHING JOB

BLOWN OUT OF BED BY BLARING BUGLES

TARGET FOR INOCULATION-HAPPY MEDICS

The classic tribulations of an Army rookie are lampooned in a series of photographic montages syndicated by King Features during the Second World War.

CIVVIES TO KHAKIS: THE MAKING OF A GI

Fresh from civilian life, millions of young Americans who had never attempted to execute the manual of arms or been exposed to the wrath of a fire-eating first sergeant or marched to anybody's cadence but their own were inducted into the U.S. Army during World War II. Going into the Army then carried an impact all its own, for America had been at peace for almost a quarter of a century, and most American men were total strangers to military life and discipline.

Green, terrified, and accustomed to his privacy and individuality, the young rookie was in for a series of jolting experiences as soon as he was sworn in. He had said goodbye to his mother, his wife or his girl friend and now found himself in an environment where, as the soldier-author of the time, Marion Hargrove, put it, "persecution is deliberate, calculated, systematic." Or so it could seem during "processing." Here, in a routine as inhuman as an industrial production line, the rookie was first fingerprinted and given a physical, then interviewed, clothed and assigned to a training company. He also received a fitting welcome from grinning regulars: "Hello, sucker!" Later, at the barber's, he lost in 50 seconds what might have taken years of careful grooming to produce.

"Home" was now a barracks, where beds standing in double rows had to be made tightly, neatly and quickly; where all worldly goods were stored in foot- and wall lockers; and where there were no partitions between toilets. Food, though there may have been enough of it, was a far cry from home cooking.

In the ensuing weeks, the recruit fell heir to the whole range of GI woes—everything from being blasted out of bed by predawn bugles to toting a full field pack on morning marches. He learned how to strip and reassemble a rifle blindfolded, gut the "enemy" with a bayonet, even lob hand grenades with the precision of a pro quarterback. "It was tough to learn how to do that stuff," one veteran later said of his own training. But during the process flab turned to muscle and a U.S. fighting man emerged.

At Fort Douglas in Utah, solemn-faced recruits file off arriving buses and get ready to form ranks upon the command of a sergeant (lower left).

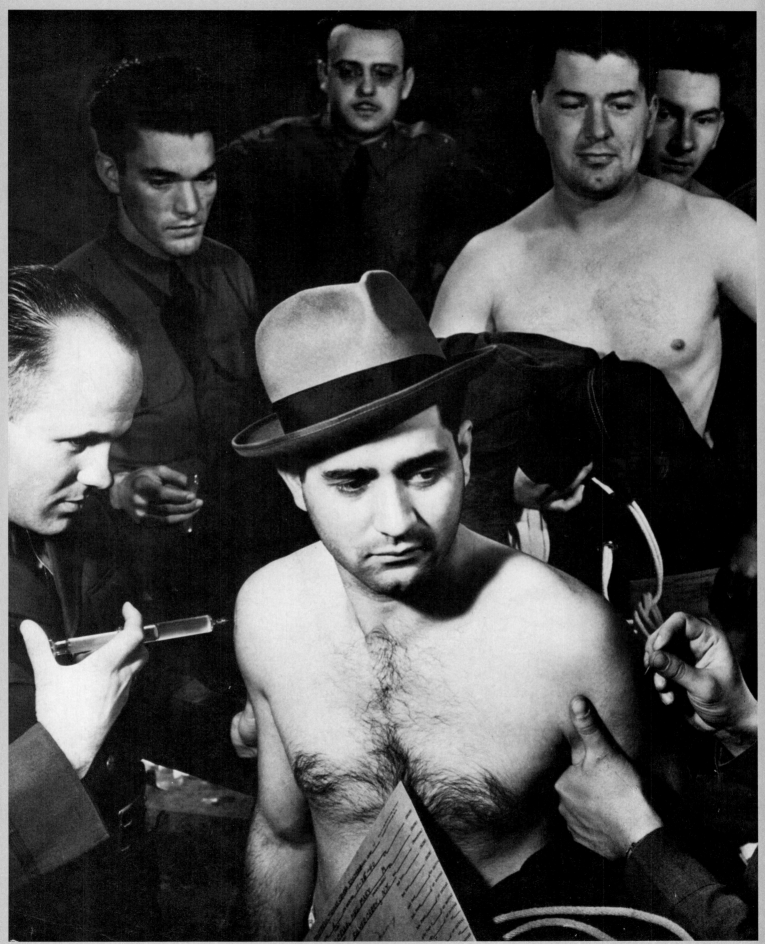

During processing, a draftee at Fort Dix, New Jersey, whose hat is now his sole claim to dignity, is inoculated from both sides for smallpox and typhoid.

Grinning troops at Camp Shelby, Mississippi, wait their turn to be sheared of their locks by one of their buddies. GI haircuts were dubbed "chili bowls."

CLIPPED HEADS AND LONG JOHNS

As the rookie quickly learned, the Army had a reason for everything. Whether the reason made sense or not was a different matter. He was obliged to forfeit two thirds of his hair for "cleanliness and sanitation," even though he was perfectly capable of taking care of it himself.

To get his shoe size, he had to hold two buckets of sand weighing 50 pounds, or as much as his marching pack. When his bare foot spread under the added weight, that was his "correct" size as far as the Army was concerned. One new man complained that he wore a size 9, not the 10½ that was issued to him. But the Army fitter would have none of it. "These shoes are to walk

in," he retorted, "not to make you look like Cinderella."

Still, each man wound up well clothed, if not always well fitted. Included in his basic issue were three suits of khakis, two wool winter uniforms, two sets of fatigues, two pairs of shoes, four pairs of socks, five suits of summer underwear and two sets of winter ones.

Describing his two-piece regulation long underwear, Private Hargrove commented sarcastically: "The undershirts are cut on a sweat-shirt pattern and are form fitting enough to send any Hollywood designer into frenzies of envy. The nether garments, which are called 'shorts' for some unfathomable reason, look like the tights worn in medieval days and show off the shapeliness of the masculine leg to best advantage—or otherwise."

A rookie at Fort Sheridan, Illinois, is measured for long johns while still in his overcoat. During the winter months, long underwear did double duty as pajamas.

A somber-looking draftee displays all of his equipment for a full field inspection. The 1917 helmet and the Springfield rifle began to be replaced in 1941.

LEARNING AND LIVING BY COMMAND

A draftee's first three weeks in the Army, dubbed the "hardening period" by veterans, were the roughest. It was the time when every private felt he had two left feet and every sergeant would agree with him. Blistered soles were common, and a good laugh was hard to come by.

Besides drilling endlessly and standing innumerable humiliating inspections, the men found themselves subjected to grueling work details. They stoked fires, hauled trash and pulled KP. One private, describing his morning misery, wrote: "We have nothing to do until 7:30 so we just sit around and scrub toilets, mop the floors, wash the windows and pick up all the matchsticks and cigarette butts within a radius of 2,000 feet of the barracks."

After a hard day's work, many wanted just to relax. Some shot pool or played cards. Others spent their free time reading, or talking and eating at the PX. And almost everyone dreamed of a weekend pass.

A sergeant shows rookies at Fort Slocum, New York, how to tuck in their ties for an A-1 appearance.

Sitting atop milk crates, dungareed soldiers on KP at Fort McClellan, Alabama, peel a sack of spuds using the time-honored knife-and-concentration method.

His basic training a thing of the past, a sergeant enjoys dancing with his girl friend at the USO, or United Service Organization, in Washington, D.C. Soldiers stationed close to smaller cities were not as fortunate. Instead of excitement and girls, most found little to do in the nearby towns but bowl, have a few beers and catch a movie before returning to camp.

Whiling away free hours at Iron Mountain, California, GIs watch a film on a makeshift screen in the desert. For morale purposes, movies were shown on a regular basis at most Army posts in everything from ordinary theaters to winterized circus tents that could seat 2,000 soldiers.

THE DISTAFF SIDE

Limp rookies contrast with two crisp officers (far right) as Director Oveta Culp Hobby reviews a training unit of the Women's Army Auxiliary Corps.

VOLUNTEERING FOR A MAN-SIZED JOB

American men were not the only ones jolted by the harsh reality of Army life. A number of women got a good taste of it, too. On the hot, sticky morning of July 20, 1942, the first volunteers—440 officer candidates and 330 auxiliaries, or privates—rolled into Fort Des Moines, Iowa, to begin training in the Women's Army Auxiliary Corps, forerunner of the Women's Army Corps, or WAC, established in 1943. Eventually more than 143,000 women served in the WAC, the largest of the women's services in World War II. Releasing badly needed manpower for the firing line, they did everything from repairing trucks to making aerial surveys—in all, more than 235 different Army jobs.

Recruiting began on May 27 and the response was overwhelming: more than 13,000 women stormed registration centers across the country. College girls, career women, secretaries, housewives and widows applied; even an Indian woman in tribal dress. So great was the turnout in Washington, D.C. *(left)*, that embarrassed officials ran out of application blanks twice during the day. In New York, 1,400 women stood in line for more than eight hours to sign up.

"If the guys can take it," one volunteer said of her new life in uniform, "so can I." This remark was no idle boast. The women took the usual inoculations in stride; a sheepish GI stood by with smelling salts just in case they were needed, but in most cases they weren't. Like all rookies, the women endured the assembly-line issuance of ill-fitting uniforms (they were too narrow in the hips and rode up the thighs), and they joked about the "rich mud-brown color" of their regulation slips and panties. They stood reveille every morning and trained rigorously all day. Many drilled in the evenings or studied Army manuals in the lighted latrines of their barracks after taps. For some old-line officers and enlisted men, the idea of women in the service—or "Wackies"—was a bitter pill. But at least one 25-year veteran disagreed. "They're a damn sight better than we ever expected they would be," said Colonel Don C. Faith, who commanded Fort Des Moines. "I honestly didn't believe they could do it."

Women volunteers line up in Washington, D.C. On the first day of recruiting, 750 showed up—more than three times the number expected.

After arriving at Rock Island Railroad Depot, Iowa, women bound for Fort Des Moines get ready for their first ride in an Army truck. Officer candidates trained for six weeks at the camp—which was the first of five training centers for women to open across the country—while the auxiliaries underwent a four-week-long course.

New arrivals, some of them already in uniform, emerge from the Fort Des Moines clothing warehouse, toting hefty duffel bags full of regular GI clothing and equipment, as well as two girdles and three brassieres each.

Beaming trainees are served soup on one of their first trips through a chow line. The women ate standard GI fare, but the calorie content was reduced on the theory that they burned up less energy than men.

An Army sergeant escorting arrivals lends a helping hand with some of their suitcases. As part of their training, the women were given the same initial instruction as men—how to properly make a bed, how to care for their own clothing and equipment, and "fall out" and "fall in."

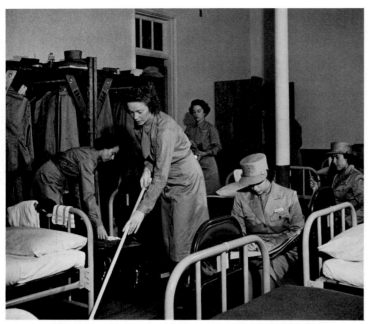

The threat of inspection produces a flurry of activity. In standard two-story barracks like this one, which housed 30 women on each floor, cots were placed head to foot to reduce the chance of spreading colds.

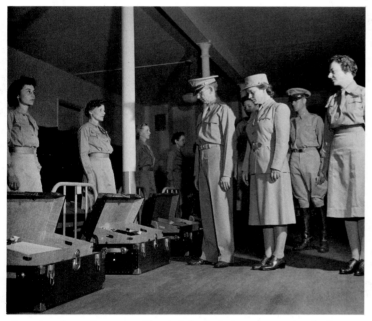

Apprehensive trainees stand by their beds during an open-footlocker inspection by Colonel Faith (left center) and Director Hobby. Personal items filled the top tray; issued underwear was stored underneath.

Hundreds of trainees do a waist-bending exercise during calisthenics at Fort Oglethorpe, Georgia. In another exercise, which was designed to strengthen arches, each woman had to pick up a pencil with her toes.

Agile women skillfully navigate a wooden obstacle at Fort Oglethorpe. Training given for overseas assignment also included descending 30-foot cargo nets and crawling through a barrage of tear-gas grenades.

Coveralled students of a motor-transport class line up in front of their vehicles in the Fort Des Moines motor pool. Women learned how to drive in convoy as well as how to free mired trucks and assemble engines.

A HARD NEW LIFE IN AN OLIVE-DRAB WORLD

The women trainees did not find themselves pampered. Although they did not handle weapons or undergo tactical training, they endured the same rigid regimen that the men did, with much the same results—aching muscles and sore feet. And they had to put up with a lack of privacy, too. At one post, the women discovered that their barracks, like all Army barracks, had no shades on the windows. At others, they encountered latrines with only makeshift cardboard partitions.

No less unnerving were the visits of inspecting officers—dubbed "bloodhounds in the boudoir" by the women—who scrutinized everything from the straightness of stocking seams to hairdos. There was, of course, KP and the daily ritual of calisthenics. And when the women were not sweating their way through gas-mask drills, they were hiking around the countryside or learning to "survive" in the field. They dug slit trenches, even bathed out of helmets. Later, in training to go overseas, they clambered over mazelike obstacle courses and took long hikes in the rain.

Through it all, the women managed to preserve their dignity and neatness—beauty parlors were set up on post and sufficient irons were issued for pressing easily creased uniforms. They also managed to have fun. For four hours in the evenings and for a day and a half on weekends, they were on their own. And like soldiers everywhere, they "did the town."

Before a contingent of visiting officers at Fort Des Moines, well-drilled women—now proud veterans of the training grind—pass smartly in review. Rookies in the

bleachers watch how it is done (right rear). Drilling went on for at least an hour a day, sometimes during snowstorms, but it offered a respite from dull classes.

3

In March 1941, bulldozers began clearing woodlands on the banks of a lazy creek 27 miles west of downtown Detroit for construction of a mammoth new Ford Motor Company building. In the next six months, the building's planners would use up five miles of blueprint paper a day, and 25,000 tons of structural steel would be consumed. When completed, at a cost of $65 million underwritten by the federal government, the barnlike edifice covered 67 acres and was aptly described as "the most enormous room in the history of man." Nearly a quarter of a mile wide and half a mile long, it was so large that errands had to be run by motorcycle or automobile.

Called Willow Run, after the creek on which it was located, the new building was the largest aircraft factory in the world designed to produce long-range bombers, B-24 Liberators, at the rate of one every hour. The manufacture of the bombers, as conceived by the Ford Motor Company's production chief, Charles E. Sorensen, called for an orderly series of steps. Raw materials would be fed into one end of the building; components made in adjacent areas would then be joined together on four main assembly lines; these would converge into one line at the other end of the structure, where the completed planes would be rolled outside onto concrete runways and flown off.

Almost from the start, however, there were huge problems. Some were technical: the B-24 had 100,000 parts as compared with 15,000 in a Ford, and in the first year of production the Army Air Forces ordered 575 major design changes, each of which required the retooling of machines.

An even more critical problem was keeping the machines manned. Willow Run had been selected as a site before the imposition of gasoline and tire rationing. Because there was little housing in the immediate area, more than half of the workers had to commute from Detroit, an hour each way. The daily absentee rate ran as high as 17 per cent, three times the national average, and the turnover was appalling: during one month, Willow Run hired 2,900 workers and lost 3,100. The personnel policies of the company's cantankerous founder, 79-year-old Henry Ford, did not help. He was bitterly antiunion, banned smoking on company time and refused to hire women for factory jobs.

Even after he relaxed the rules, the plant still was beset with personnel problems. By the end of 1943, the elaborate

MIRACLES OF PRODUCTION

assembly-line setup was turning out only one bomber a day, and people across the country were joking that Willow Run's name should be changed to "Willit Run?"

At the government's urging, Ford began to decentralize the mammoth operation. Much of the equipment used to manufacture parts for the B-24 was farmed out to other Ford plants and to subcontractors. The scaled-down work force could now focus on the assembly-line operation, the pivotal point of Sorensen's original concept. Decentralization produced dramatic results. By 1944, a B-24 was rolling out of Willow Run every 63 minutes. In all, the plant produced 8,685 Liberators, capable of delivering up to four tons of bombs apiece each time they roared over enemy territory.

The planes that rolled off the assembly line at Willow Run were only part of an avalanche of armaments produced by American industry during World War II. Before that conflict came to an end, American plants turned out 296,429 airplanes, 102,351 tanks and self-propelled guns, 372,431 artillery pieces, 47 million tons of artillery ammunition, 87,620 warships, 44 billion rounds of small-arms ammunition—in all, $183 billion worth of war materials. So impressive was this feat that even such a grudging admirer of American achievements as Russian Premier Josef Stalin proposed a toast at the Teheran Conference late in 1943 "to American production, without which this war would have been lost."

America's role as the great armaments maker of World War II began a year before Pearl Harbor. "We must be the great arsenal of democracy," President Roosevelt said in a fireside chat, calling upon America to supply its allies—and build up its own defenses—with planes, tanks, guns and ships. But harnessing the industrial might of the United States and turning it from civilian production to war output required a massive governmental effort. Only the government could effectively decide priorities, award contracts, allocate scarce materials. The task, gargantuan in itself, was further complicated by the traditional American aversion to government "meddling" in private enterprise. Businessmen accustomed to freewheeling did not take kindly to dictates from Washington bureaucrats, let alone the baffling regulations and the reams of paper work they generated.

The government's solution was to employ the old carrot-and-stick technique. The stick was the power to deny such

critical materials as steel and aluminum to producers of items deemed nonessential to the defense effort. The carrot was the prospect of profits to be gleaned by converting to the manufacture of essential goods. As Secretary of War Stimson baldly put it in the privacy of his diary: "If you are going to try to go to war, or to prepare for war, in a capitalist country, you have to let business make money out of the process or business won't work."

The money to be made was alluring indeed. The no-risk arrangement devised by the government—and known far and wide simply as "cost plus"—guaranteed the holder of a defense contract not only funds to cover his costs but a hefty profit as well.

The cost-plus policy took effect during the pre-Pearl Harbor defense build-up and soon incurred the wrath of a peppery United States Senator, Harry S. Truman of Missouri. In late 1940, he began receiving complaints from constituents about waste in the construction of Fort Leonard Wood, an Army camp in the southern part of his state intended to house thousands of the new draftees. Truman decided to see for himself. One wintry day he got into his broken-down Dodge and drove from Washington to the camp, arriving unannounced.

What he saw there made his blood boil. Building materials of all kinds were out unprotected in the snow and rain, "getting ruined, things that could never be used, would never be used. Some of them had been bought because somebody knew somebody. . . . And there were men, hundreds of men, just standing around and collecting their pay, doing nothing."

Truman had been an artillery captain in World War I, serving under fire in France, and he was all for government spending that would help the soldier's lot in any way; but he also expected the government to get its money's worth. He was especially incensed at the huge fixed fees assured to cost-plus contractors regardless of what they had been charging for their products before the War. The government, he concluded, was handing out these profits "in much the same way Santa Claus passes out gifts at a church Christmas party."

After visiting Fort Leonard Wood, Truman drove more than 25,000 miles to other camps and to defense plants around the country, finding evidence of millions of taxpayers' dollars going down the drain. Upon his return to Washington, D.C., he called for the establishment of a special Senate watchdog committee, a move that was warmly endorsed by his colleagues. In March of 1941 the Special Committee to Investigate the National Defense Program came into being, with Truman as its chairman. Until he resigned in order to run for the Vice Presidency in 1944, he was to remain the relentless scourge of such misusers of government funds as makers of defective airplane parts and cheaters who lied about the tensile strength of the steel plate that they produced.

Shoddy workmanship would never be completely eliminated, of course. Some American weapons and equipment proved faulty: improperly welded Liberty ships that broke apart, guns that jammed, torpedoes that did not explode. But thanks in considerable measure to Truman and his investigators, these failures were exceptional; moreover, by the War's end, the committee's sleuthing had saved the country an estimated $15 billion.

The bungling and the waste that Truman and his colleagues uncovered were far from one-sided. The government itself was to blame for much of the trouble in the defense program. The businessman who admitted that, "if it

hadn't been for taxes, we couldn't have handled our profits with a steam shovel" was offset by others who were more altruistic and sincerely eager to pitch in to help the cause of democracy. Many of them went to Washington on their own to seek a contract—only to find the capital a mind-boggling maze of rival agencies and divided authorities. A supposedly all-powerful new Office of Production Management, for example, did not have the final say-so over the awarding of contracts; that was up to such long-entrenched agencies as the Army-Navy Munitions Board and the Maritime Commission.

More often than not, small businessmen bidding for a share of the defense effort found themselves out in the cold, and anything but impressed with what they had seen of the capital. "Washington's a funny town," one frustrated petitioner fumed. "It's got scores of hotels, and you can't get a room. It's got 5,000 restaurants, and you can't get a meal. It's got 50,000 politicians, and nobody will do anything for you. I'm going home."

The industrial giants fared better than the small businesses—and not only because of their proven ability to produce on the mass scale that the military required. They enjoyed added influence through company men who were

in the capital serving in the government for a dollar a year, but who often retained their corporate salaries and loyalties. A survey made in December 1942 showed that 71 per cent of all defense contracts were held by America's 100 biggest corporations.

Yet in spite of the certainty of great gain, many of the nation's business leaders were at first wary of plunging into the defense effort. After the Depression of the 1930s, the economy had just begun to flourish again, releasing a pent-up civilian demand for automobiles, refrigerators, vacuum cleaners, luxury gadgets. Eager to exploit this growing market, manufacturers foresaw only the headaches that would be involved in retooling their plants and coping with ever-shifting military specifications. Moreover, no one could be sure how much longer the war in Europe would continue; Hitler appeared to be on an irreversible winning streak. In the postwar era, overexpanded plant facilities could be a costly burden.

The prudent course for American manufacturers was to take on some military orders but at the same time keep turning out a cornucopia of consumer goods. This attempt to resolve the classic dilemma of guns versus butter was doomed to failure: arms production during the prewar period fell far short of the government's goals. It took the rude awakening of the catastrophe at Pearl Harbor to put America's war machine into high gear.

The Japanese attack touched off a nationwide clamor for a single director of the war effort—a "czar" empowered to do whatever was necessary to get things done. Some of the men around Roosevelt had been urging such an appointment for many months, but the President's preferred way was to spread responsibilities so diffusely that it was seldom clear who was in charge—except himself. Even his supporters conceded that he was no genius as an administrator. "The boss," said one, "either appoints one man to do four jobs or four men to do one. Often he does both."

One day in mid-January, 1942, more than a month after America's official entry into the War, Roosevelt received two successive visits that helped change his mind about a czar. One visitor was Harry Truman. As a freshman Senator in 1934, he had been obliged to wait five months before getting in to see Roosevelt for just a brief social call; now, as

the increasingly prestigious chairman of a Senate investigating committee, he had access to the White House at will. What he had to say to Roosevelt this time was short but not sweet: his committee was about to issue its first annual report, and it would indict the war production effort as an unholy mess.

Following Truman into the Oval Office was Wendell L. Willkie, the Republican Presidential candidate in 1940. He had come armed with an impressive personal statistic. He had counted up, he told Roosevelt, and found that he had publicly called for a single director of the war effort 87 times during the campaign and 37 times since. That night, Willkie went on, he planned to make his 125th try in a speech before an audience Roosevelt could not afford to shrug off—the United States Conference of Mayors.

Willkie did not have to make the 125th try. Later that afternoon a big, affable Missourian named Donald M. Nelson arrived at the White House, summoned from a meeting of the government's Supplies, Priorities and Allocations Board. As the SPAB's executive director, Nelson was already in the top ranks of Washington's wartime hierarchy; even so, he was stunned to learn of the elevated post that Roosevelt had in mind for him. He was to be head of a new War Production Board (WPB), with more authority over the nation's economy than any other American except the President himself.

In discussing his marching orders with Roosevelt, Nelson politely reminded the President that previous so-called superagencies had failed because neither their functions nor their powers had been adequately defined; he would need, he said, an Executive Order spelling out his role. The President's reply was typically breezy. "He told me," Nelson recalled, "to write out my own order and send it over to him; he'd sign it."

Drafted by Nelson, with the help of his advisers, the order was unprecedented in scope. Nelson was no power-grabber; he was, in fact, somewhat abashed by his sudden press acclaim as a "dictator" about to "tackle the biggest job in all history." But he was a thoroughgoing pragmatist. To do the job, he required, and got, the authority to commandeer materials and assign priorities in their use, compel the conversion and expansion of plants and bar the manufacture of products he judged to be nonessential. Moreover,

Production czar Donald M. Nelson climbs down from an armored vehicle in July 1942, while Chrysler president K. T. Keller (left) and plant manager E. J. Hunt (center) look on. Industry-wide conversion from cars to war production had recently been completed, and Nelson was in Detroit to give defense workers a pep talk. Their job was just beginning, he told them; in 1943 the U.S. would count on them to turn out $12 billion in war matériel—nearly nine times their output in the previous six months.

his orders were to take precedence over those issued by any other government agency.

At 54, Nelson had come a long way since his boyhood in the little Missouri town of Hannibal, made famous by Mark Twain; once, while taking a piano lesson in Twain's old house, he had even met the great author when he dropped in for a nostalgic look around. Nelson's own youthful aspirations were academic; he had hoped to become a professor of chemistry. Instead, he had gone to work for Sears, Roebuck, rising to become its $70,000-a-year executive vice president in charge of merchandising.

How this qualified him to supervise history's biggest production job was a mystery to many people in Washington; Nelson himself long remembered the "polite coughs and lifted eyebrows" that greeted his elevation. But, as he pointed out, the Sears, Roebuck experience was invaluable. Responsible for procuring 100,000 different items, from spools of thread to fertilizers to heating equipment, he had been compelled to learn a lot about their methods of manufacture in order to know where to find them at the right price. As WPB boss, he was to retain a merchandiser's eye. When he saw Winston Churchill at a White House meeting wearing a one-piece siren suit, he was instantly reminded "of a pair of the overalls which we had sold in great quantities at Sears, Roebuck & Co. to filling-station operators and

to mechanics who had to crawl underneath automobiles."

Offsetting Nelson's strengths was a major weakness: his distaste for contention. In spite of his dictatorial powers, he preferred to rely on persuasion and amicable compromise, patiently hearing out all sides of a dispute, his plump and untroubled face reminding one observer of a "Middle Western Buddha."

Nelson's mild manner posed a problem with respect to the awarding of contracts. Though nominally he had the control, he chose to leave this vital matter to the military. The military, chafing in any event under civilian direction, was not especially grateful, and some observers thought Nelson was too easygoing with the brass. "One of these War Department generals," a Nelson aide remarked, "will stick a knife into Nelson, and all Nelson does is pull the knife out and hand it back and say, 'General, I believe you dropped something.' "

But beneath his affable exterior Nelson was to prove tougher than some of his critics suspected. In the weeks that followed the WPB's creation, a stream of edicts flowed from his office sharply curtailing or entirely banning the production of approximately 300 items judged to be nonessential to the war effort. Among them were refrigerators, bicycles, waffle irons, beer cans, toothpaste tubes, coat hangers—even metal caskets. The manufacturers of these products were given a hard choice: they could convert to essential items, or they could try to find and make do with substitute materials.

For consumers, the worst blow was the word that they would have to get along without new cars for the duration. In four decades, Americans had grown used to the picture of Detroit as a boundless purveyor of pleasure on wheels; since 1900, almost 86 million automobiles and trucks had rolled off its assembly lines. But now those assembly lines—the core of the mass-production system that would be the key to victory—had to be preempted. Predictably, the mandatory conversion of the automobile industry was among Nelson's first edicts. No other industry could produce with the speed and in the volume required in wartime. In the end, it was to turn out $29 billion worth of war matériel.

The wheeled and tracked vehicles of war were obvious candidates for manufacture by Detroit, and they came off the lines in staggering numbers: a trainload of tanks every

The boarded window of an electrician's shop in Coolidge, Arizona, proclaims—somewhat optimistically—the fate of one small business in 1942. Facing shortages and giant competition that they could not keep up with, many such businesses had to shut down—and in doing so changed a traditional American fact of life. At the beginning of the War, some 175,000 small companies did 70 per cent of the nation's business; by March 1943, however, they accounted for only 30 per cent.

day, 2.4 million military trucks in all. There was also a strange new conveyance, the amphibious DUK-W, better known as just plain "duck." Half truck and half boat, the duck could lumber through the water transporting 50 soldiers at a speed of 6.4 mph, then clamber ashore and make as much as 50 mph on the highway. It was used with great success in the invasions of Sicily and the mainland of Italy, and in a string of amphibious operations in the Pacific that included Tarawa, Kwajalein and Saipan.

The most popular wartime vehicle to come out of the auto industry was the rough-riding jeep, made by Willys-Overland and by Ford. Equipped with four-wheel drive, it could travel cross-country and just about anywhere else. The only bone of contention about the jeep concerned the origin of its name. Some people claimed that the name

came from the odd animal character in the comic strip *Popeye;* the government insisted that it was a corruption of the official designation—GP for "general purpose" vehicle. Josef Stalin took such a fancy to the jeeps he received via Lend-Lease that he kept asking for more of them, although Russia's dictator did nothing to dispel the Red Army myth that they were Soviet-made—produced in a secret factory beyond the Ural Mountains at a place improbably called "Willys-Overland."

The techniques used to turn out vehicles also proved adaptable to the mass production of weaponry of every sort. Chrysler, for example, tackled the manufacture of the Bofors 40mm antiaircraft gun, which had from one to four barrels capable of extremely rapid fire. The Swedes, who had developed the Bofors, required 450 man-hours to make

A PAIR OF THE WAR'S MOST VERSATILE VEHICLES

Two of the most ingenious vehicles turned out by workers on the home front were the jeep and the amphibious DUK-W, or duck.

The jeep proved as nimble as a motorcycle and was able to negotiate rocky hills, marshy swamps and shifting sands. Originally designed for messenger service, it was soon being put to dozens of other uses in every war theater. With an antitank gun in tow, it could quickly bring firepower to bear on enemy armor or, with a litter attached, evacuate wounded off the battlefield. It was variously called the iron pony, leaping lena and panzer killer. Brigadier General Theodore Roosevelt, son of President Teddy Roosevelt, and an assistant division commander in North Africa, Sicily and France during the War, affectionately named his jeep Rough Rider.

The jeep's less widely sung but equally heroic cousin, the duck, had its two-and-a-half-ton truck chassis encased in a watertight hull fitted with propeller and rudder for duty in water. The duck gave a new dimension to landing operations. Transport ships could anchor out of range of beach-based guns, open their bows, lower their ramps and disgorge hundreds of ducks that ferried troops and cargo ashore and then carried them inland at speeds up to 50 mph. About 1,000 ducks took part in the invasion of Sicily in 1943; more than twice that number participated in the Normandy landing the following year.

A jeep bounds over the crest of a hill, yanking a 37mm antitank gun behind it.

Troops roll overland in a duck, which by a flick of a lever could be converted to sea duty.

one gun by handcrafting. Chrysler's engineers designed jigs, dies and other machine tools to mass-produce the parts, which could then be put together on the assembly line; total manufacturing time was 10 hours.

By the summer of 1942 the auto makers were also heavily involved in the manufacture of airplanes, engines and other aircraft parts. While Ford was ironing out the production problems at Willow Run, the Packard Motor Company was making Rolls Royce engines for the RAF, Chrysler was manufacturing bomber fuselages, and General Motors was assembling fighters and turning out wings, landing gear and other parts for bombers.

But the aircraft production goals set by President Roosevelt required a gigantic effort, and the major burden would have to be borne by the aircraft industry itself. In the 32 years between the Wright brothers' pioneer flight and the start of the defense build-up in 1940, U.S. aircraft manufacturers had produced a total of 75,000 planes by the use of handcraft methods. The President was calling for 60,000 planes in 1942, and 125,000 in 1943.

Within a few weeks of the Pearl Harbor attack, six billion dollars in planes and aircraft equipment were on order. Fulfillment of these orders would require an enormous enlargement of production potential, and the aircraft industry set about at once to increase its plant capacity. The Boeing Airplane Company began expanding in the Seattle area; Douglas Aircraft enlarged its facilities in Southern California to include a new $12-million plant at Long Beach. Bell Aircraft put up a new fighter assembly plant at Niagara Falls, New York, and a huge new bomber factory at Marietta, Georgia. Across the country, the number of aircraft plants increased from 41 in 1940 to 81 in 1943, while floor space for plane manufacture and assembly was expanded from 14 million to 170 million square feet.

Employment in the aircraft industry rose from 100,000 in 1940 to over two million at the peak of the war effort. Although President Roosevelt's goal of 125,000 planes in 1943 proved unattainable, the total U.S. production increased from 23,000 planes per year before Pearl Harbor to 85,898 in 1943 and 96,318 in 1944.

Moreover, as the War progressed, the quality of American aircraft improved dramatically. The performance of the B-17 Flying Fortress and the B-24 Liberator, the work-horse bombers of the Army Air Forces, was improved: the B-17's speed was increased from 256 to 287 miles per hour, and its range was extended from 1,377 to 2,000 miles; the B-24's speed and range remained about the same, but its armament was dramatically increased. Before the end of the Second World War the B-17 and B-24 were superseded by the B-29, the gigantic Superfortress. Almost twice as large as its predecessors, the B-29 could travel a third farther and faster and carry over two and a half times the bomb load. U.S. fighters also improved dramatically from the sluggish P-40 Tomahawk widely used at the outset of the War to the swifter, more agile P-38 Lightning, P-47 Thunderbolt and P-51 Mustang, generally regarded as the finest fighter of World War II.

To meet America's stupendous production goals a special breed of industrial leader was required. Men were needed to hack their way through jungles of red tape, improvise solutions to production problems and inspire their employees to herculean efforts. Of all the miracle workers, the most dynamic, perhaps, was the shipbuilder Henry J. Kaiser. A landlubber who persisted in calling a ship's bow the "front end," Kaiser built nearly one third of America's 2,716 Liberty ships—the ungainly-looking merchant vessels that bore the brunt of carrying matériel to the fighting fronts. Kaiser's very name became a synonym for getting things done fast and effectively.

He had been in a shipyard only once before he started building ships. But to this new pursuit he brought organizational genius and the techniques he had perfected in the construction industry. A junior-high-school dropout, he began his career as a photographer and paving contractor, and went on to construct the San Francisco-Oakland Bridge and the world's largest dam, the Grand Coulee. During the War, Kaiser operated seven shipyards and revolutionized shipbuilding. Instead of laying a keel and constructing the ship around and above it by riveting, he had sections prefabricated and then welded together. His methods were so effective that at the peak of the War he astounded the world by building and launching a ship in only 80 hours and 30 minutes.

Kaiser was a 260-pounder with energy to match his physique. In his early sixties, he slept only four hours a night, spent $250,000 a year in long-distance phone calls and rushed around the country hiring workers, organizing new projects and cutting government red tape to get priorities for steel and other materials. When his shipyards ran short of steel, he borrowed $106 million from the government and built California's first steel mill, near Fontana. Kaiser, said an associate, "is like a breathless elephant. He just leans on you, smiles, and you move."

The industrial giants such as Kaiser and Ford usually got what they wanted, but in the scramble for materials many small companies fell by the wayside. Some were elbowed out in the competition for scarce metals; the little fellow whose product required just a bit of copper, for example, stood no chance when the War Production Board's own experts were having to juggle the dwindling supply for use in munitions, in the ships and trains to move them, and in the electric transmission lines to power the arsenals where they were made.

Businessmen who were lucky enough to secure a hearing could not always be sure of a logical reaction from the WPB's bureaucratic thinkers. One food processor requested a priority for materials to construct a 100-foot-long conveyor belt. When a WPB official asked what proportion of the company's production went into the war effort, the reply was "60 per cent." The official did some quick figuring and ruled that the company could have priority for a conveyor belt just long enough to match that proportion—60 feet.

Priority ratings, when obtainable, proved to be a particular source of discouragement to small businessmen. The WPB started out simply with the ratings A, B and C, but applicants who managed to wangle an A soon found that it had been topped by ratings AA and AAA—granted independently of the WPB by the military's chief contracting agency, the Army-Navy Munitions Board. Henry Kaiser himself took a dim view of the system. "A priority," he said, "is something which gives you an option to ask for something which you know you're not going to get anyhow."

Kaiser could cut his way through the labyrinth of the WPB; smaller fry tended to get lost. In less than a year Nelson's domain had 25,000 employees and a stupefying table of organization that included such units as the Pipe, Wire Products and Galvanized Steel Jobbers Subcommittee of the Iron and Steel Advisory Committee.

The howls of the modest entrepreneurs quickly reached Capitol Hill. In mid-1942 an act of Congress required the War Production Board to set up a Smaller War Plants Division "to mobilize aggressively the productive capacity of all small business concerns." Later reorganized as a corporation with lending powers, it was headed by a former Texas Congressman, Maury Maverick, who liked to live up to his name. A passionate foe of bureaucracy, Maverick was destined to win a permanent place in the dictionary by coining the word "gobbledygook" to decry bureaucratic jargon; his own memos were labeled with such trenchant phrases as "bloody urgent."

Maverick championed the cause of the small businessmen, securing prime contracts and subcontracts for thousands of them. But the battle was never fully won. Many would-be participants in the war effort had to shut down; by 1942, there were 300,000 fewer small companies in existence than there had been before the War.

All told, some 200,000 companies—large, medium and small—successfully made the conversion to war production. Some were able to take the leap with relative ease. A bedspread manufacturer turned to making mosquito netting for use in tropical combat zones. A soft-drink maker, accustomed to filling bottles with liquids, instead loaded shell casings with explosive chemicals. A producer of rubber boots now made pontoons. A paper-box manufacturer

A New Jersey man implements his solution to the tire shortage in 1942—a retread made from soles of old shoes. Rubber was one of the most critical—and scarcest—of wartime materials: a Flying Fortress took half a ton, a destroyer some 50 tons. Military needs for the 18-month period beginning in July 1942 were estimated at 842,000 tons—200,000 more than in the national stockpile. Not until mid-1944 was there enough synthetic rubber to ease the shortage and again allow civilian consumption.

turned out plasma kit containers. One typewriter company went back to its own roots, on one side of the corporation, at least. L. C. Smith had started out in the 19th Century by fashioning shotguns, and later merged with Corona in the typewriter business. Now the merged company turned to producing rifles.

For other manufacturers the transition was more difficult, involving the use of unfamiliar machines and techniques. A maker of model trains switched to bomb fuses, a merry-go-round manufacturer to gun mounts, a casket factory to airplanes, a piano factory to airplane motors, a pinball-machine producer to hardware for parachute harnesses.

The requirements of mechanized warfare compelled the creation of some new industries, most notably as a result of a perilous shortage of rubber. In early 1942, when Japan's seizure of Malaya and the Dutch East Indies cut off 90 per cent of America's imports of natural rubber, the United States had less than a year's supply on hand—and the needs were increasing: a B-17 Flying Fortress required half a ton of rubber, and U.S. tanks used a ton.

One potential source of natural rubber was the guayule plant, which grew wild in the Southwest and in Mexico, and which, in fact, had provided half of America's rubber supply in the early part of the 20th Century. An attempt was made to cultivate guayule on a large scale, but the harvest was too slow to count on.

A second potential source was reclaimed scrap rubber. In June 1942, Roosevelt called on the public to turn in "old tires, old rubber raincoats, old garden hose, rubber shoes, bathing caps, gloves." In New York City, a carload of chorus girls from a Broadway musical drove up to one collection depot, Nat Jupiter's service station, and wriggled out of their girdles. In Washington, Secretary of the Interior Harold L. Ickes spotted a rubber floor mat at the White House, rolled it up and had his chauffeur deposit it at the nearest collection point. Within four weeks Roosevelt's appeal brought in some 450,000 tons of scrap rubber. But much of it, like Ickes' floor mat, already had been reclaimed at least once and was unsuitable for further reprocessing.

Finally, Roosevelt imposed nationwide gasoline rationing—more to conserve rubber than gas—and ordered full-steam-ahead on synthesizing rubber from petroleum, a process in which the Germans had a huge head start; they had undertaken it in the 1930s. The American government spent $700 million to build 51 synthetic-rubber factories, then leased them to private industry. By 1944, the factories were producing 800,000 tons a year—the equivalent of the harvest from 180 million rubber trees.

A few manufacturers performed the neat trick of persuading Washington that their regular peacetime product was essential to the war effort. The classic case involved Wrigley's chewing gum. To stay in business, Philip K. Wrigley had to solve two formidable problems: the lack of chicle, which, like rubber latex, had been coming from trees in Japanese-occupied Southeast Asia, and the shortage of sugar, which was rationed in the United States. Wrigley overcame the first obstacle by turning to South America, where chicle trees grew abundantly. He had his gum-tree tappers there tap rubber trees growing in the same areas. He then arranged to have the chicle transported back to the States in ships carrying the high-priority rubber. Next, to obtain a sugar priority from the government, Wrigley needed to demonstrate that his chewing gum was essential to the war effort. He argued—with the help of a government laboratory—that chewing gum was a great reliever of wartime tension; he wound up not only supplying a stick of gum for each package of the Army's combat K rations, but packing the rations in his factory as well.

Chewing gum was thus to become, along with such other American stand-bys as chocolate bars and cigarettes, the common currency for GIs who bartered their way across foreign soil. Wrigley also distributed his product to war plants, with this skillful sales pitch: "To help your workers feel better, work better, just see that they get five sticks of chewing gum every day."

The civilian labor force that was ultimately responsible for the wartime triumph of American technology was the most productive in the nation's history—and the most unusual.

Operating at full blast, industry had to rely heavily on the skills of those who had been largely excluded from the factories in prewar days: women, blacks, Southern white migrants, teenagers, convicts and ex-convicts, the aged and the physically handicapped. At San Quentin prison in California, inmates turned out matériel ranging from antisubmarine nets to night sticks for the National Guard. In Maine a builder of wooden minesweepers lured 100 ship carpenters out of retirement, including one man aged 84, after discovering that no one else knew how to use an old-fashioned tool called an adz. Aircraft plants hired midgets to inspect the cramped insides of plane wings, blind workers to sort out rivets from the floor sweepings. Other factories hired the deaf for jobs in plant areas where the high noise level was intolerable to people of normal hearing. Many states suspended their child-labor laws for the duration; by mid-1943, some three million youngsters aged 12 to 17 were employed in war work.

Unemployment virtually disappeared. Even those who in ordinary times chose to remain idle wound up with jobs. Urban police rounded up skid row inhabitants, weeded them out for useful skills and offered suspended sentences to those in trouble with the law—if they would go to work. In 1942, when Jeff Davies, president of Hoboes of America Inc., filed his customary annual report with the State of Indiana, he disclosed that virtually all of the two million members had left the road. Many were in the service and

the rest had jobs. The few exceptions were not full-fledged hoboes at all, Davies added—"They're just bums."

Though most of the newly employed had never seen the inside of a factory, new training techniques and the relative simplicity of mass-production methods reduced the need for long apprenticeships. Henry Kaiser's shipbuilders, for example, shortened the training period required for a welder from three months to just 10 days. In fact, workers with few skills sometimes fared better on the assembly lines than those with a high degree of training. Former watchmakers had to be retrained because of their distressing tendency to stop the assembly line and repair faulty parts instead of throwing them out.

How-to manuals came into their own. For the B-29 alone, the Boeing Airplane Company published half a dozen manuals, totaling more than 2,000 pages. When a high government official visited Boeing's plant in Wichita, Kansas, and questioned the need for all those manuals, an Army Air Forces colonel who was showing him around staged a convincing demonstration. He picked an employee at random and had him study the Boeing *Pilot's Handbook* for five minutes. Then the employee climbed into the cockpit of a B-29 Superfortress, compared the maze of dials and throttles with the illustrations in the book and 18 minutes later had all four engines running.

The most significant addition to the wartime work force, the more than six million women who took jobs *(pages 88-101)*, came relatively late. Factory managers had been loath to hire women, arguing that they did not understand machines and, moreover, would distract male workers. In 1941, when Vultee Aircraft took the plunge and hired 25 women for production jobs, it rushed them to work on March 31—a day earlier than planned—lest the experiment be branded an April Fool's joke.

In the first six months after Pearl Harbor, an estimated 750,000 women applied for work in war plants, but only about 80,000 were taken on. With a growing shortage of manpower, however, industry was forced to reconsider, and an intensive recruitment of women began. Radio stations, newspapers and magazines exhorted women to "enlist" at their local employment office. Posters showing Lockheed Aircraft's mythical "Rosie the Riveter"—a buxom, long-lashed heroine in coveralls—began appearing everywhere,

In Valparaiso, Indiana, junkman Frank Schumak vainly defends a 200,000-pound pile of scrap that military policemen have come to appropriate. Schumak, claiming he wanted the metal as an investment for his old age, had refused to sell it at the government's price of $18.75 a ton. But such holdouts were rare. Three weeks after the government called for scrap drives in mid-1942, civilians had contributed five million tons of pots and pans, horseshoes, discarded car bumpers and other metal objects.

along with feature stories about her real-life counterparts. "If you can drive a car you can run a machine," became the slogan of a Connecticut ordnance plant's campaign to hire 5,000 more women.

The addition of women to the work force was not only essential for production, but also evidence of the all-out effort on the home front. The traditional picture of the all-American girl with the toothy smile was supplanted by the image of a dirt-streaked face beneath hair bound up in a bandanna. Military photographers were often assigned to factories to get that morale-boosting new image to relay to the forces overseas.

It was on such a mission that an Army photographer named David Conover discovered a curvaceous 19-year-old beauty at the Radio Plane Parts Company in Burbank, California. When Conover spotted her, she was spraying a liquid on the fuselage of a plane and radiating an uncommon mixture of sex appeal and ethereal beauty. Her name was Norma Jean Baker, and she agreed to pose for Conover only after he had secured written permission from her foreman. Conover spent three days taking pictures of her around the plant—in the overalls she normally wore to work and also in a sweater. One of her pictures appeared in the Army magazine *Yank* and came to the attention of a photographer named Potter Hueth, who in turn photographed her and showed his pictures to a modeling agency. Under the name of Marilyn Monroe, she would wind up one day making movies.

The presence of women in the war plants helped improve working conditions, bringing such innovations as employee cafeterias and decent rest-room facilities, as well as the addition of such labor-saving devices as mechanical lifts to the assembly lines. Employers became more aware of the need for safety precautions; industrial accidents were causing more American casualties than the fighting itself. Safety goggles were made mandatory for certain operations and protective guards were built into machines.

Women might have gone into war work in even greater numbers except for a variety of deterrents. One was a current myth that a job on an assembly line could cause all sorts of bodily ailments, including a mysterious malady called "riveter's ovaries," which supposedly resulted from excessive vibration. A bigger deterrent was the matter of unequal pay. Though men liked to joke about it—"Remember when women had to get married to get men's wages?"—the fact was that even now the wages paid to women averaged about 40 per cent less than those earned by men doing the same jobs. The government's War Labor Board ruled that women should receive equal pay for equal work, but it left too many loopholes. General Motors, for example, simply changed its separate categories of male and female workers to "heavy" and "light" and went on discriminating in its pay scales.

The most serious deterrent for many women, however, was the fact that a factory job only added to their domestic burdens. More than 50 per cent of the female work force were full-time housewives, saddled with the continuing need to shop, cook and care for the children. Many women also had trouble finding transportation to work. What one company labeled "the DTs"—domestic and transportation difficulties—led to a high rate of turnover and absenteeism. The turnover rate at Boeing was so high that, over a four-year period, the company had to hire 250,000 women in order to maintain a work force of 39,000. When one woman was questioned as to why more members of her sex did not go into war work, she snapped: "Because they don't have wives."

Absenteeism—both female and male—was a persistent concern in the war plants. In 1943, with absences from the job running as high as 20 per cent in some plants, the flying hero Captain Eddie Rickenbacker undertook a one-man crusade across the nation. "There is no absenteeism in the foxholes in the jungles of the Pacific or the burning sands of Africa," he declared, "for if attempted there, they would get a bayonet in their bellies from their fellow Americans." Some industries used lotteries and other cash incentives to keep people at work every day, while women employees of a Portland shipyard hit upon their own effective solution:

they refused dates with fellow workers who were absent without good cause. Soon, other companies followed suit and started "No work—No woo" clubs.

Strikes proved less of a threat to war production. Shortly after Pearl Harbor, labor leaders took a no-strike pledge, and for the most part they lived up to it. Overall, strikes cost less than half of 1 per cent of all work time, and any labor dispute that did erupt made headlines.

The most notorious involved a series of strikes in 1943, by approximately 400,000 coal miners who were demanding higher wages. Their leader, John L. Lewis, a burly man with a silvery gray mane, beetling black eyebrows and a gift for rolling Biblical rhetoric, was by far the most colorful figure in the American labor movement. Lewis detested Roosevelt and was ready to take on all of Washington. When the government took over the struck coal mines and threatened to operate them with soldiers, his defiant answer was: "You can't mine coal with bayonets." Soon, critical shortages of coal developed along the East Coast, eliciting from Interior Secretary Ickes one of the worst puns of the War: "We can fuel all of the people some of the time, and fuel some of the people all of the time. But in war we can't fuel all of the people all of the time."

For a time, Lewis was probably the most unpopular man in America. Polls showed that though a majority of the people thought the miners deserved a raise despite wartime wage ceilings, 87 per cent regarded Lewis unfavorably—a feeling shared by the fighting men. "Speaking for the American soldier," said an editorial in the GI newspaper *Stars and Stripes,* "John L. Lewis, damn your coal-black soul."

The miners' strikes, eventually settled after a small wage increase, brought demands that all strikers be drafted and revived discussion of a national service law, similar to Britain's, that would enable the government to assign people to whatever jobs it deemed necessary. In January 1944, Roosevelt called for such a law in his State of the Union message, but neither business nor labor wanted it. Nor did most women. "A woman kept on any job . . . against her will is likely to act like a cat on a leash," declared the head of a women's organization. "Don't forget that a man may have the strongest *will,* but a woman has the strongest *won't.*"

Most employers devised their own answers to the problems of labor disputes and absenteeism. Many got around government wage ceilings by introducing such fringe benefits as medical insurance. Jack and Heintz Precision Industries, Inc., a Cleveland company producing airplane parts, gave monthly banquets for employees, provided free Turkish baths and referred to all of its 9,000 workers as "associates." Andrew Jackson Higgins, a swashbuckling Louisiana manufacturer of torpedo boats and landing craft, relied on an unabashed appeal to his employees' patriotism. He had "The Star-Spangled Banner" played over loudspeakers and had pictures of Hitler, Mussolini and Hirohito posted in the men's rooms, with the caption: "Come on in, brother. Take it easy. Every minute you loaf here helps us plenty."

The workers themselves spurred on one another through sheer pride of craftsmanship. Engineers at a plant in Newburgh, New York, made what they thought was the finest steel wire possible, stretched so thin that it was almost invisible. They sent it to a rival factory upstate with the note, "This is just to show you what we are doing in Newburgh." A few weeks later the wire came back mounted on a steel block with a small microscope attached. One by one the engineers peered through the microscope, chagrined to find that their rivals had succeeded in boring a minuscule hole in the wire.

For workers with ties to the men on the battlefronts—the fathers, mothers, brothers, sisters and wives on the production lines at home—there was a special incentive that outweighed everything else: the possibility that their own handiwork might somehow directly affect the life of a loved one. They relished the story of a seaman named Elgin Staples, whose ship went down off Guadalcanal. Staples was swept over the side, but he survived, thanks to a life belt that proved, on later examination, to have been inspected, packed and stamped back home in Akron, Ohio, by his own mother.

HEROINES OF THE HOME FRONT

Painters line up for action at a Newark, New Jersey, shipyard. Though barred from shipyards before the War, women held 10 per cent of the positions by 1944.

TAPPING THE NATION'S WOMANPOWER

America's war effort called for an augmented labor force large enough to fill not only those vacancies left by men who had gone into the service, but also new jobs created by urgent wartime needs. To bring this force up to strength, the nation looked to its women.

Only one thing stood in the way: ingrained prejudices about women's place in society. The government got together with industrial leaders and persuaded the bosses that if the War was going to be won, they would have to overcome their male biases. An advertising campaign was instituted. Billboards aimed at women posed such provocative questions as, "What job is mine on the Victory Line?" and supplied some ready answers: "If you've followed recipes exactly in making cakes, you can learn to load shell." The women responded. By 1943 they constituted nearly a third of the total work force. Among those who did not take jobs, many managed to make a contribution of another kind through volunteer work.

Some women, like New York commercial designer Josephine von Miklos, sacrificed their regular lives and comfort to the war effort purely out of patriotism. "To hell with the life I have had," von Miklos wrote in 1943. "This war is too damn serious and it is too damn important to win it." Closing her New York studio, she took a job in a New England munitions factory. Down South, the 80-year-old widow of Confederate General James Longstreet turned her back on the benefits of retirement and joined the 8 a.m. shift at the Bell Aircraft factory in Marietta, Georgia.

Still, prejudices about women in industry died hard. Some people argued that women lacked the ability and stamina to perform jobs previously held only by men. Jokes reflected the surprise that people felt in discovering that women could indeed hold such jobs. One cartoon showed a girl at a finishing school saying, "I flunked in charm and social composure, but I passed in welding and riveting." By the time the War ended, doubts were fewer, and most Americans were willing to concede that victory could not have been achieved without the contribution of the women.

A Vermont woman holds down a Victory store vegetable counter in 1942. Proceeds from the sale of donated produce went to buy military supplies.

Working on the railroad, two women take a break from their task of wiping down locomotives in the San Francisco yards of the Southern Pacific in 1943.

A Red Cross volunteer serves lunch from a mobile canteen at an Army post near Washington, D.C.

Fire brigade volunteers in Port Washington, New York, clamber aboard a fire truck in a practice drill.

OUT OF THE KITCHENS INTO THE WAR EFFORT

Of the millions of women who joined the war effort, the greater number were unpaid volunteers who gave of their own time to perform vital services on the home front. And no one was too old or too young to participate in one of the many volunteer programs. Two thousand girls in Tennessee pooled their efforts to harvest a million gallons of strawberries, and in one New England community three alert septuagenarian women gladly took turns on a round-the-clock civilian-defense plane-spotting detail.

Many women found that they could put to use some of the talents and skills they already possessed. More than three million joined the Red Cross to run canteens or serve as nurse's aides or drive ambulances. And more than one million others provided food, entertainment, company and good cheer for lonely servicemen at USO centers across the nation.

For women who knew that they wanted to do something, but did not know exactly what, there was an abundance of advice from a variety of sources. "Should your mentality lean toward maintaining law and order," suggested one call-to-action publication in 1942, "you can become a volunteer police clerk."

Civilian-defense workers monitor communications at a center in Philadelphia. Many women also served as couriers, air-raid wardens and fire watchers.

A NOT-SO-SUBTLE DIFFERENCE IN ROLES

Women who took paying jobs soon demonstrated that there was almost no limit to the kind of tasks they were prepared to do. Rolling up their sleeves, they went to work driving steam rollers, garbage trucks and taxis. In Los Angeles one of the first female hearse drivers and casket bearers at Forest Lawn cemetery said proudly: "I'd even dig graves if I had to, and it may come to that." In the Northwest, 4,000 women in logging handled jobs as varied as whistle punks, tallymen, flunkies, bull cooks and lumberjacks—who wound up being labeled "lumberjills."

The best-paying jobs were in war industry. To make up for the women's lack of experience, many firms offered on-the-job training in welding and riveting and such specialties as the operation of giant cranes. Soon women were doing everything from cutting tool dies to loading shells and assembling airplane fuselages. And, in the end there was only one major difference between what they did and what the men did—pay. The women earned less.

Taking up where the men left off, two aproned women hose down animal carcasses in an Albert Lea, Minnesota, packing plant. After the War, this unpleasant job reverted to men.

A Fremont, Nebraska, farm girl carries a bucket and an automatic milker on her way to milk the farm's eight cows, a twice-a-day chore, while the hired hands are in the service.

A young woman from Philadelphia becomes accustomed to grease as she works on a vehicle's undercarriage at the Atlantic Refining Company in 1943.

THE ODD REQUIREMENTS OF DEMANDING JOBS

The demands of a full-time job in heavy industry were more than just physical; women had to adapt their dress and habits to a working environment and a schedule that allowed little time for normal shopping, homemaking and supervision of children.

On the job, the women were obliged to wear practical clothing. Some companies hired leading designers to create stylish work uniforms, but most simply required female employees to don slacks and sturdy shoes. Long hair posed a threat, especially the shoulder-length "peekaboo" hairdo made popular by movie actress Veronica Lake, which could be lethal if caught in the gears of a machine. Employers appealed to Miss Lake to set an example by changing her peekaboo trademark. She adopted an upswept hairstyle, and her career soon went into eclipse. Most working women solved the problem of what to do with their hair by putting it up in bandannas or gathering it in protective net snoods.

Unfortunately, all problems were not so easily solved. Among the more difficult and frustrating were shopping and caring properly for the kids while holding a job on a shift. Department and grocery stores stayed open late to meet the needs of working women. And the federal govern-ment, after much equivocation, helped to build and operate some 2,800 child-care centers, but the number was sufficient for less than 10 per cent of the children of working mothers.

Whatever problems women faced and however they solved them, they still managed to do their jobs with aplomb. When the men returned home from the War, anthropologist Margaret Mead wrote, they would find women "more interchangeable with men than they used to be, better able to fix a tire, or mend a faucet or fix an electric light connection, or preside at a meeting, or keep a treasurer's account, or organize a political campaign, than when they went away."

A woman operating a vertical lathe at the Alameda, California, Naval Air Station in 1942 wears appropriate attire—heavy shoes, a slack suit and a bandanna.

Factory welders in Connecticut wear their protective masks at the ready. The *number of black women in industry rose by 11.3 per cent during the War.*

A 23-year-old worker in a steel mill in Gary, Indiana, directs the movement of a huge ladle used for molten iron to the transfer car she operates at left.

Assembly-line workers at a Midwestern munitions plant turn out 37mm antitank shells. They were among 31,000 women employed in plants manufacturing shells

and small-arms ammunition in 1942. Because the wages averaged 40 per cent higher than those offered in most factories, women flocked to this high-risk job.

4

In the early days of the War, when antiaircraft weapons were being hurriedly set up in some American cities, a Seattle cabdriver complained because soldiers had placed a machine gun in his backyard. "My kids won't stay away from it, and my wife is going nuts," he said. "Funny, ain't it? The Navy wouldn't have me, the Army couldn't use me, and now they've gone and brought the goddam war right to my kitchen door."

Before long the War was not only at the kitchen doors of America but also inside the living rooms, the schools, shops and movie theaters. Although the cities of the United States were never bombed and no invading army ravaged the countryside, home-front Americans knew very well that there was a war on. They were reminded of it every day by a whole range of new and unfamiliar experiences: taking part in air-raid drills, coping with shortages and rationing, planting vegetable gardens, buying War Bonds, collecting scrap metal and accepting heavy doses of propaganda in their entertainment.

Daily life on the home front changed in both tempo and quality. In households where the alarm clock used to go off at 7 a.m. it now clanged at 6 a.m. People had to rise earlier to get to the office or plant on time; gas and tire rationing foreclosed the luxury of driving one's own car to work and compelled the use of jam-packed buses, trolleys, commuter trains or, at best, car pools.

Breakfast was no longer the hearty repast with which Americans traditionally fortified themselves against the day ahead. Eggs were plentiful, but a strip or two of bacon on the plate now represented a dubious expenditure of treasured meat-ration stamps. Rationing also dictated a less lavish slathering of butter on the toast, a more judiciously measured teaspoonful of sugar in the coffee and second thoughts about the need for a second cup. The mere act of getting breakfast required conscious care: since kitchen appliances could not be replaced, slamming the refrigerator door or overtaxing the toaster or electric percolator became a risky matter.

With breakfast over, the house emptied of all but the very old and very young. As often as not, the wife-and-mother joined the exodus. The prewar stereotype of the woman in frilly apron, bidding her spouse goodbye as he set forth on his daily joust as sole family breadwinner, vanished from

BRINGING THE CONFLICT HOME

the American scene. With her husband away at war—or even if he was deferred and still at his peacetime pursuits—a woman who clung to the usual housewifely routine was regarded as old hat.

Everywhere she turned, a woman's services were much in demand; all manner of jobs were hers just for the asking (pages 88-101). Propelled into the working world by patriotism and the lure of extra income, she experienced there the heady satisfactions of being away from pots and pans and radio soap operas, of making new friends and broadening her horizon.

And there was another, more somber incentive. The one desperate and largely unspoken fear that haunted people on the home front was the possibility of receiving a telegram from Washington reporting the death or wounding of a loved one in battle. Keeping as busy as possible left less time for brooding over this prospect.

As a result, few women seriously complained of a way of life that required constant juggling. Taking on a job did not relieve them of the necessity to clean the house, do the laundry, cook and shop—racing to the butcher's when rumors spread of the arrival of a new shipment of rationed meat, often having to queue up to buy it. The children posed another problem: working mothers had to arrange for someone to keep an eye on the kids after school. Day-care centers were as yet a rarity; the usual solution was to enlist the vigilance of a neighbor or relatives. Sometimes the older folks moved in—or made room in their own home for the married daughter and her youngsters. Shared living quarters were a common phenomenon; under the exigencies of wartime, members of the first, second and third generations—each with their own duties and responsibilities—discovered that they could, after all, get along under the same roof.

A new kind of camaraderie also flourished in offices and factories. People pulled together more than before; loafing on the job, jockeying for favor, indulging in petty intrigue suddenly seemed puerile and irrelevant. Clothes became a great leveler; informality of dress was the rule, even in ultraconservative firms. Secretaries unselfconsciously wore slacks. Their male co-workers sported unmatched jackets and trousers. A woman who owned a pristine Shetland sweater, or a man who boasted a little-worn all-wool suit, begrudged using it now for everyday wear; with wool going into military uniforms, such items were hard to come by in the stores.

Indeed, shopping for just about anything was a test of skill. Lunch hour turned into a marathon search for the most mundane of objects, especially anything made of metal. Bobby pins were scarce; so were can openers, flashlight batteries and other household dependables previously taken for granted. And the scramble for whatever was available was keen; store aisles were jammed with shoppers bent on the same quests.

A pause for a sandwich or a bowl of soup on the way back to work could be equally vexing; sometimes it seemed as if every restaurant in town had a long waiting line—with no guarantee of decent service inside. Complaints about the slowness of service or poor quality of the food brought the inevitable surly rejoinder from overworked waitresses: "Don't you know there's a war on?"

After the struggles of the day, other problems awaited at home at night. Feats of cookery had to be improvised. Chicken, though never in short supply, had to be varied one more time. A creditable applesauce cake could be produced with the prudent use of carefully hoarded fat. Dishes had to be washed, empty cans set aside for the scrap collection. Only when the children were in bed was there time to sit down—in a living room that was made gloomier by blackout curtains and chillier by a thermostat set at no more than 65°.

The adults might relax over a book, Chinese checkers, a word game or a rubber of bridge; going out to a movie, unless it was within walking distance, meant expending precious gasoline. Most people preferred to save that for a Sunday spin, visiting relatives or friends or rediscovering the local zoo—an alternative suggested by zoo officials in place of gas-guzzling weekend trips. But after a bone-wearying work week—the 48-hour official minimum was often exceeded—long-distance travel did not appeal very much in any case.

Sometimes, before dropping off to sleep, the home-front American would count up the disruptions and inconveniences of the day and feel a tingle of annoyance. But that would be fleeting; after all, everybody else was enduring them. More often there was a sense that coping represented a contribution to the war effort, an awareness that life, as never before, had a direction and a purpose.

Americans on the home front were forced to accept a degree of regimentation and government interference in their lives that they would not have tolerated in peacetime. The pursuit of the government's war objectives gave rise to a welter of official federal agencies known by sometimes-bewildering acronyms, like the OPA (Office of Price Administration), OWI (Office of War Information) and OCD (Office of Civilian Defense).

The OCD, which had been formed seven months before Pearl Harbor, was the principal government agency for channeling the energies of the people on the home front. Its first director, Fiorello H. La Guardia, called on Americans to contribute "an hour a day for the U.S.A." A flamboyant five-foot-two dynamo, La Guardia was valued more for his promotional flair than for his abilities as an administrator. He could devote only part of his time to the job because he was already Mayor of New York City, where he delighted his constituents by wearing a black sombrero and personally leading police raids. On the day the Japanese attacked Pearl Harbor, he raced around the city in a siren-blaring police car screaming "Calm! Calm! Calm!" Two days later, while La Guardia was on the West Coast organizing civilian-defense forces, an erroneous report of approaching enemy planes led to an air-raid alert in his home city. To the Mayor's embarrassment, most New Yorkers paid no attention to the wailing sirens except to pause briefly and gaze up at the sky.

The OCD's main job was to get sky-gazing citizens off the streets and protect them in the event of an air attack. To this end, the agency prepared mass-evacuation plans and recruited millions of volunteers to serve as airplane spotters, air-raid wardens and ambulance drivers. Practically every community in the United States was organized right down to the block level, where the air-raid warden was in charge of keeping all lights turned off during the periodic night-time blackouts. Air-raid wardens were authorized to wear white helmets and arm bands and carry whistles. But in the early days of the War there was an equipment shortage, and wardens in New York had to enforce the blackouts with dime-store whistles that were stamped "Made in Japan."

The same shortage of equipment forced communities to improvise their own air-raid warning devices. Reading, Pennsylvania, used a symphony of automobile horns—three short blasts and a long, corresponding to the three dots and a dash in Morse code that stood for V as in Victory. In Sepulveda, California, a 100-year-old cast-iron bell was rung as a warning device. Finally, the Bell Telephone Laboratories, working under a federal contract, developed a standard model Victory Siren. Powered by an automobile engine, the siren generated a blast that covered an area 10 miles square and was said to be capable of breaking eardrums at a distance of 100 feet. It was so loud, in fact, that many communities refused to buy it, and the Army briefly considered using it as a combat weapon.

When no air raids materialized, some Americans began to consider blackouts a nuisance and cooperated only under threat of a fine. In New York's suburban Westchester County, citizens were so blasé about blackouts that civilian-defense authorities tried to make compliance a matter of religion by promoting hymn singing and prayer during air-raid alerts. Authorities in Sheridan, Wyoming, had a more practical solution for making certain all the lights would go out: they designated as the town's blackout chief the head of the local electric company.

For many, however, the blackout was a rewarding ritual. It became a time for patriotic introspection, a way of feeling an emotional link with the battlefronts and bomb-torn cities thousands of miles away. To a Chicago air-raid warden, it seemed that "the war is no longer in far-off London or Chungking." Many children of the War years relished the excitement of sitting by dim candlelight, using their hands to make flickering shadow figures on the wall, and enjoying the romantic and mysterious sense of impending danger that the blackout conveyed.

The physical precautions against air attack were minimal. Many cities kept boxes of sand and pails of water on street corners for use against incendiary bombs. But a shortage of building materials prevented any large-scale program of bomb-shelter construction. The White House bomb shelter in the basement of the Treasury building was supposed to be a secret. But a Roosevelt-hating Republican Congressman, Clare E. Hoffman of Michigan, gave it away by placing in the *Congressional Record* a description of the room and its location. In Hollywood, Jack Warner did not bother with a bomb shelter for his movie studio even though a prime potential target, the Lockheed Aircraft factory, was practically next door: he simply had a set painter inscribe a 20-foot arrow on the roof of a sound stage with a sign announcing in large letters, "LOCKHEED THATAWAY."

In the absence of bomb shelters, citizens were advised to make do. A civilian-defense pamphlet titled "What to do in an air raid," which was distributed to 57 million Americans, suggested that "the safest place in an air raid is at home." It advised readers to lie down under "a good stout table," having prepared beforehand by laying in a large stock of supplies. In Manhattan the Brearley Nursery School adapted the latter advice to its special needs. A notice to members of the staff stated: "The Nursery School will keep on hand an adequate supply of food, blankets, first-aid equipment, flashlights and lollipops."

The Office of Civilian Defense encouraged its volunteers and others to take first-aid training. The best-selling book of 1942 was the *Red Cross First Aid Manual,* which sold no fewer than eight million copies. Volunteers practiced their

splinting and bandaging on spouses at home and then, during air-raid alerts, displayed their skills on "victims"— Boy Scouts, groaning enthusiastically and splashed with tomato ketchup to simulate wounds.

Cities vied with one another for the status of being first on the enemies' hypothetical list of targets. In Illinois, one civilian-defense pamphlet showed that Chicago was closer via the polar route to German-occupied Norway than was New York City. Though rational people recognized that no land-based enemy planes had the range to reach the U.S. and return, there was fear that Axis pilots might attack and then bail out. A *Colliers* magazine editorial pleaded with "any civilians who may reach these airmen ahead of police or soldiers not to obey the human impulse to lynch them, shoot them, or kick them to death." In fact, even one-way trips from the nearest enemy-occupied territory were impossible, and Japan would have had to risk valuable aircraft carriers to get within striking distance of the West Coast. There was never any real threat of large-scale bombing of American cities.

The U.S. *was* bombed, but only after the initial air-attack scare had faded. On September 9, 1942, Flying Officer Nobuo Fujita of the Imperial Japanese Navy climbed into a Zero that had been carried across the Pacific in a special watertight compartment of a submarine and was catapulted into the air off the West Coast. Navigating by the glare of a lighthouse that had not been blacked out, he crossed the shore and dropped two incendiary bombs on a forest region in Oregon. The aim of the mission was to set off a fire storm that would sweep down the coast, but the flames quickly sputtered out. Fujita flew back to the submarine in his pontoon-equipped plane and on September 29 tried again. Again the forest failed to ignite. The only enemy pilot to bomb the U.S. in World War II gave up and went home.

Much later in the War—at the end of 1944 and the beginning of 1945—the Japanese did manage to cause casualties and damage in the U.S. with bombs carried not by airplanes but by balloons. Thousands of large paper balloons, each carrying several 30-pound bombs timed to explode from three to five days after launching, were released in Japan to ride the high-velocity stratospheric air currents across the Pacific. The balloons were ingeniously designed

Mayor Fiorello H. La Guardia reviews a detail of New York City policemen at an air-raid drill in 1943. He held frequent city-wide drills, complete with mock fires, broken water and gas mains, and make-believe accidents. La Guardia—who served as head of the Office of Civilian Defense between May 1941 and February 1942—often turned up to direct the drills.

to dip groundward, drop a single bomb and soar up again to distribute the rest of their loads across the Western United States. Approximately 300 of the balloons managed to reach the U.S. and Canada, and their cylindrical missiles set several fires and took six lives.

Ironically, most of the American public, having been geared up for possible air raids by blackouts and the wailing of sirens, had no knowledge of the balloon bombs until after the War was over. The federal government clamped a censorship lid on the balloon story to prevent the Japanese from finding out that the balloons were even partially effective. Unaware of their small success, the Japanese abandoned the project.

The most serious threat in the early days of the War was the German submarines that were sinking Allied freighters within sight of the Atlantic beaches. Hunting U-boats was, for the most part, a job for Navy and Army aircraft. But the Office of Civilian Defense developed an antisubmarine weapon of its own—the Civil Air Patrol. The CAP was formed to make use of pilots who were overage or otherwise not eligible for the military. Serving without pay, the CAP's 40,000 part-time volunteers flew their own light aircraft on missions such as ferrying military passengers and mail, and dropping mock bombs—sacks filled with flour—on factories to demonstrate the vulnerability of American industry. Beginning in July 1942, armed with real bombs, they undertook submarine-patrol duty in the Atlantic. The CAP was so effective—it bombed 57 subs and was credited with several kills—that in 1943 the Army snatched it away from the OCD's jurisdiction.

The Office of Civilian Defense, in addition to guarding the home front, had been entrusted with a second mandate: enrolling civilians in community activities, such as health, welfare, child care and physical fitness, that were less clearly related to the war effort than bombing U-boats or enforcing blackouts. For this purpose the OCD created a Volunteer Participation Division. La Guardia, who was convinced the U.S. would be attacked at any moment, considered this second mandate "sissy stuff"; as a consequence, two months after Pearl Harbor his agency found itself embroiled in a dispute with Congress.

La Guardia had chosen as director of the Volunteer Participation Division a very determined woman named Elea-nor Roosevelt. Although her husband was the President, Mrs. Roosevelt was an imposing force in her own right; for one thing, her syndicated newspaper column, *My Day*, was probably the most widely read feature in America. Mrs. Roosevelt plunged into her new job with characteristic zeal. She proclaimed a national "Dance-for-Health-Week" and personally led lunch-hour folk dances in the corridors at OCD headquarters.

She also made two appointments that quickly became centers of controversy. One was the actor Melvyn Douglas, an outspoken liberal, to head the division's Arts Council. The other was a ballroom dancer named Mayris Chayney, an old acquaintance of hers, to be chief of the Children's Activities Section of the Physical Fitness Division. In 1938, Miss Chayney had introduced a new dance step in honor of the First Lady and called it "the Eleanor Glide." Her new job was to develop programs of dancing and rhythmic exercises that could be performed in air-raid shelters.

To a Congress already in a sour mood because of discouraging news from the Pacific battlefronts, Melvyn Douglas' appointment was bad enough. Some congressmen darkly accused the actor of "Communist tendencies." But the appointment of a dancer gave them the opportunity for a field day—especially after they discovered that the Physical Fitness Division employed no fewer than 62 coordinators for such unwarlike sports as quoits, horseshoe pitching and table tennis. They mocked Mrs. Roosevelt's appointee as a "fan dancer" and "a strip teaser" and, in the unkindest cut of all to the First Lady, passed a rider to OCD's appropriations bill in February 1942 that prohibited the use of federal funds for "instruction in physical fitness by dancers, fan-dancing, street shows, theatrical performances or other public entertainment." Melvyn Douglas and Mayris Chayney resigned. So did Eleanor Roosevelt, probably to her husband's relief.

Meanwhile, La Guardia, who had been under fire from the beginning because he was a part-time director, also resigned. He was succeeded by James M. Landis, dean of the Harvard Law School and a former New Dealer whose precise and humorless legal mind yielded up the following formula for achieving a blackout: "Such obscuration may be obtained by the termination of the illumination." This

THE HOME FRONT'S ONLY CASUALTIES

A balloon and its bomb hang down from telephone wire in California.

During the War, Japan sent thousands of balloon-borne bombs to the U.S. via high-altitude air currents blowing across the Pacific. Of the 300 that reached the West Coast of the U.S. and Canada, a few drifted as far as Iowa and Kansas. Most failed to go off, and only one caused casualties. The fatal bomb landed on Oregon's Mount Gearhart, where the Reverend Archie Mitchell had taken his wife and five parish kids on an outing. While Mitchell parked the car, the others searched for a campsite. On the way they came upon the bomb on the ground; it exploded and killed all six.

In August 1943 the Reverend Archie Mitchell and his wife posed for a wedding picture. Two years later, she was killed by a Japanese balloon bomb.

meant, as the President dryly pointed out at a press conference, "turn off the lights."

Under Landis' regime nearly 1,000 town meetings were held all over the U.S. as a testament to American unity and to step up recruitment of volunteers for civilian-defense activities. These meetings, supposedly spontaneous, were carefully stage-managed by OCD officials. In Northport, Alabama, where townspeople were summoned by the Mayor riding like Paul Revere on a horse through the streets, 2,000 residents turned out, of a population of 2,500. By mid-1943, the nationwide civilian-defense corps had reached a peak strength of more than 10 million volunteers.

As fears of enemy air attack waned, the OCD's other activities took on more importance. For example, the agency encouraged discipline and self-denial—"Every time you decide *not* to buy something, you help to win the war." It urged families to make themselves into "a fighting unit on the home front" and earn the "V-Home Certificate" by conserving food, salvaging essential materials, buying War Bonds regularly and refusing "to spread rumors designed to divide our Nation."

Civilian-defense volunteers played an important role in the home front's vast scavenger hunts—campaigns to collect scrap materials for recycling into armaments. Every community had a scrap drive of some sort going on almost all through the War, and very little escaped the collector's net. Junk steel and other metals were obviously of value, but so were such lowly disposables as bacon grease (used in the manufacture of ammunition) and old silk and nylon stockings (used to make powder bags for Naval guns).

"Slap the Jap with the Scrap" was the theme song, though Bing Crosby came up with one entitled "Junk Will Win the War." In Boston a black-tie benefit on behalf of the scrap drive brought in a Civil War Gatling gun and the Governor's rowing exercise machine. In Wyoming a group took apart an old 20-ton steam engine and then built several miles of new road just to get the scrap to the collection center. Perhaps the spirit of it all was best summed up by a variation on the title of another wartime song—a sign on an old jalopy that wound up at a government collection depot proclaimed, "Praise the Lord, I'll Soon Be Ammunition."

The most zealous collectors were the children *(pages 118-127).* At home they painstakingly peeled off bits of tin foil from cigarette packages and gum wrappers and rolled them into hefty balls, which brought 50 cents each. They pestered neighbors for everything from old rubber overshoes to tin cans, which they took delight in stomping flat.

Scrap paper—cardboard boxes, newspapers, envelopes—was the easiest junk to come by. A youngster in May-wood, Illinois, collected more than 100 tons of it during the War. One paper drive carried out by the Boy Scouts in 1942 so glutted the pulp mills that it had to be temporarily halted. The connection of scrap paper to the war effort was less apparent than that of tin cans or tin foil. The government said paper was needed for packaging the armaments that were being shipped overseas and insisted that the shortage stemmed from the lack of manpower in the lumber camps. Others blamed the horrendous proliferation of paper work in Washington.

To promote scrap-metal drives, civilian-defense officials came up with examples of what could be done with the scrap. The iron in one old shovel, it was pointed out, was enough to make four hand grenades. By the end of the War, scrap was supplying much of the steel and half of the tin needed for American weapons production. Just as important, all those collection drives helped join together home-front citizens in a morale-boosting enterprise.

The planting of vegetable gardens similarly produced both practical and psychological benefits. Secretary of Agriculture Claude R. Wickard came up with the idea of "Victory gardens" soon after Pearl Harbor, even though American farms already were producing enough to feed half the world. Planted with vegetables of every description, new gardens sprang up in backyards and the most unlikely places—the zoo in Portland, Oregon, Chicago's Arlington Race Track and a downtown parking lot in New Orleans. In 1943, Americans planted 20.5 million Victory gardens, and the harvest accounted for at least one third of all the vegetables consumed in the U.S. that year. Dietary habits changed as Americans discovered such previously unfamiliar vegetables as kohlrabi and Swiss chard. Housewives became more nutrition-conscious, canning their own vegetables and contributing to another of the government's aims for the home front—the creation of a healthy citizenry.

While the varied activities of civilian defense thus gave millions of Americans an authentic sense of participation,

other governmental programs imbued them with a sense of sharing in the sacrifices exacted by modern war. These programs—special taxes, War Bonds and rationing—all had other primary aims, but the psychological effects were significant by-products.

The tax programs and War Bond campaigns had two primary goals. One was to pay for the enormous costs of the War—more than $330 billion in military expenditures over a four-year period. The second was to fight inflation by sopping up excess wages at a time when there were acute shortages of many consumer goods. By mid-1943 the home front was awash in so much money—some $70 billion in cash, checking accounts and savings, compared with $50 billion in 1941—that one U.S. Treasury official referred to it as "liquid dynamite."

The federal government imposed a 5 per cent surcharge on all income taxes, attempting to soften the blow by calling it a "Victory tax." At the same time, Uncle Sam began requiring employers to deduct from workers' paychecks the appropriate percentage of wages due as income taxes, which hitherto had been paid once a year. This was the beginning of the withholding tax that, to this day, diminishes the paycheck of every American wage earner. The pay-as-you-go plan stepped up the cash flow to the U.S. Treasury and appreciably reduced the chances of tax cheating—a valuable accomplishment at a time when it was vital that Americans feel that everyone was pulling together.

The Treasury's other major source of immediate cash was War Bonds, which could be bought in denominations ranging from $25 to $10,000. Americans purchased some $135 billion in bonds during the War. Banks, insurance companies and big corporations accounted for much of that total, but $36 billion of it was in Series "E" small-denomination certificates that were bought by ordinary citizens. When President Roosevelt launched the program in 1941, many of his advisers had favored making their purchase compulsory. They felt a nonvoluntary program would avoid the vicious community pressures that had been applied during World War I, when citizens stigmatized those who failed to purchase bonds by painting their homes and barns yellow. But Secretary of the Treasury Henry Morgenthau—whom Roosevelt referred to affectionately as "Henry the Morgue"

Using every bit of available space in front of their home, an Oregon couple tends a Victory garden on the fringe of a Portland sidewalk. By May 1943, some 18 million Americans had planted cabbages, radishes and other vegetables at sites as various as Boston's Copley Square and Chicago's Cook County Jail—where small crops were encouraged, but corn was forbidden because it might offer would-be escapees concealment.

because of his sober banker's mien—insisted on a voluntary program. It would "make the country war-minded," he said, "and give people an opportunity to do something."

To sell the bonds, Morgenthau recruited help from Madison Avenue, comic-strip heroes and big-name entertainers. Advertisers, many of whom had lost their marketable products for the duration, donated space and radio time worth an estimated $400 million to bond drives (they were encouraged by the War Advertising Council and a federal ruling that the cost of the ads could be counted as a business expense for tax purposes). Many of the War Bond posters used scare tactics. One such poster pictured three young girls being leered at by a Nazi officer. "A high honor for your daughter," it said, suggesting that if the reader failed to buy bonds, his daughter might wind up a victim of invaders. The campaigns also provided Superman with an

opportunity to do his bit on the home front, by urging those who read his comic strip to buy bonds. Though Joe Palooka and other comic-strip heroes were in military uniform, Superman had failed his Army physical because his X-ray vision penetrated through the wall, and he read the eye chart in the next room. (Actually, his creators and syndicators had correctly figured that Superman's winning major battles singlehandedly would only make him an object of derision to frontline soldiers, so they made him 4-F.)

A series of mammoth bond rallies featured film and radio stars. Betty Grable's stockings and Man o' War's horseshoes were auctioned off in return for pledges to buy bonds. Hedy Lamarr kissed anyone who bought $25,000 worth of bonds—a prospect so overwhelming to one buyer that he fainted before he could collect, or so her press agent reported. A bond auction in Gimbel's bargain basement

offered such historical items as Thomas Jefferson's personal Bible and Jack Benny's $75 violin, "Old Love in Bloom," which brought a one-million-dollar bid from a New York cigar maker. But the champion seller of all was the singer Kate Smith, who in one 16-hour marathon on network radio sold nearly $40 million worth of bonds to listeners who called in their pledges.

The major sacrifice that was required of most people on the home front was involuntary—the unprecedented rationing of some 20 essential items by the federal government. Rationing, in combination with price controls, was aimed at equitably distributing scarce goods and at keeping a lid on inflation. The hard-to-get goods covered by rationing ranged from gasoline to tomato ketchup, and their scarcity stemmed from a variety of reasons. Canned foods, for example, were rationed because tin went into armaments and cans for soldiers' C rations, coffee because the ships that would ordinarily carry the coffee beans from South America had been diverted for military purposes, shoes because the Army alone needed some 15 million pairs of combat boots.

The first item to be rationed nationwide was sugar. In May 1942, Americans lined up at their local elementary schools, where the teachers and other volunteers took depositions as to how much sugar the consumer already had at home and then issued ration books containing coupons good for a 52-week supply. Soon the housewife's proverbially cluttered handbag was stuffed with books of ration stamps—red for meat, butter and fats, blue for canned foods such as peas or beans. To prevent hoarding, the stamps were coded so that they would be redeemable only for a specified period of time, usually a month. Meat rationing was further complicated by the fact that each cut required a different number of red stamps. What's more, the number fluctuated with the available supplies; hence, a pound of roast beef might cost one stamp one week and three stamps the next. On the average, however, each person was allowed two pounds of meat a week.

The system for rationing gasoline was even more elaborate. Each motorist was assigned a windshield sticker with the appropriate letter of priority, from A to E. If his car was used for pleasure driving only, he received an A sticker good for one stamp, which was worth three to five gallons a week; the quantities differed by region and were revised from time to time. Commuters received a B sticker worth varying amounts of gas based on their distance from work. The sticker of highest priority—E for emergency—was assigned to policemen, clergymen and, occasionally, politicians, and brought as many gallons as needed. For the most part, farmers also were granted unlimited quantities of gas, but they paid for it in the limitless amounts of paper work required by the government. One Midwestern cattle farmer became so fed up with the red tape that he wrote to his congressman demanding his own stenographer from the Civil Service. He said he was willing to pay her wages but insisted he had to have one "that can ride a saddle horse and drive a pick-up."

Rationing generally was a cumbersome operation. Each month some three billion stamps, each less than an inch square in size, changed hands. From the consumer the stamps went to the retailer, who passed them on to the wholesaler, who gave them to the manufacturer, who had to account for them to the federal government. Presiding over this accountant's nightmare was the Office of Price Administration. Although the OPA operated through some 5,500 local rationing boards, which like the draft boards were made up of volunteer workers, its bureaucracy nonetheless encompassed more than 60,000 full-time employees. Among them for a time—before he accepted a Navy commission—was Richard Nixon. He had left college a liberal, Nixon later said, but became "more conservative" after toiling in an agency that seemed to embody all the evils of bureaucratic government.

The OPA was everyone's favorite wartime scapegoat. One psychologist correctly predicted that rationing would cause frustration and produce an aggressive response. That aggression, he theorized, could then be directed against the enemy. Instead, it was most often directed toward the OPA. Citizens took great delight in blunders such as the one made by the OPA office in Philadelphia when it failed to ration sufficient heating fuel for itself and had to close down temporarily.

While the great majority of Americans confined their resentment of rationing to grumbling about the OPA, millions of others illegally circumvented the rationing laws. A black market in meat, gasoline and other rationed items flourished throughout America during the War years. The customer could have all these things if he was willing to pay the price. In Washington, D.C., "Mr. Black," as illicit entrepreneurs were called, could supply the well-heeled shopper with a pair of nylon hose for five dollars, or a pound of boneless ham for $1.25, nearly twice the ceiling price imposed by the government. In Pittsburgh, an investigative reporter armed with $2,000 in cash but no ration stamps came up with a ton of meat.

Organized crime had a piece of the black-market action. After racketeers printed and sold counterfeit ration stamps, the government tried to outwit them by printing the stamps on specially treated paper that would change color when immersed in chlorine and exposed under ultraviolet light. But the racketeers simply heisted the special paper from federal warehouses.

Even the friendly neighborhood grocer or shop owner dabbled in the black market from time to time. For a price, or out of loyalty to old customers, he could produce from under the counter a pound of steak, a can of vegetables or even a coveted chunk of the bubble gum his store was ostensibly out of.

There was some social stigma associated with cheating on the items in short supply, but rationing was so unpopular—and the black market so ubiquitous—that many people had a tendency to look the other way, much as they had tolerated bootlegging during Prohibition. By one estimate, black-market transactions accounted for more than 25 per cent of all retail business on the home front. The courts went lightly on businessmen convicted of black-market infractions, usually meting out small fines. In a Gallup poll, one out of four respondents condoned at least occasional patronage of Mr. Black.

This tolerance for what one writer has called "low-caliber lawlessness" extended to the illegal practice of hoarding goods that were about to be rationed—tires, sugar, canned food. "I'm just stocking up before the hoarders get there," was the usual justification.

For all the griping about and evasion of rationing and price controls, the OPA's program did pay off. Inflation was stemmed: in the OPA's most effective years, from 1942 to 1945, the total rise in consumer prices was only 9 per cent.

And though rationing was a daily irritant, it was also a daily reminder that the nation was at war. In fact, practically every inconvenience, every shortage, every small sacrifice—meatless Tuesdays, gasless automobiles, ketchup-less hamburgers—was justified as a contribution to the war effort.

Gas rationing, in particular, yielded other benefits. Automobile fatalities dropped dramatically—by 42 per cent during one period in New York State. A new custom called the commuter car pool came into being. And walking was back in style, to the great satisfaction of Dr. Herman Sonderling, a Long Island podiatrist who asserted that the automobile was to blame for flat feet, a major source of draft deferments. The OPA administrator, Leon Henderson, tried to set an example by riding a bicycle through Washington. It quickly turned out, however, that consumers could not buy bicycles either.

Shortages existed in thousands of different items that were never rationed, and consumers everywhere were confronted with signs exhorting them to "Use it up/Wear it out/Make it do/Or do without." Among the things shoppers could not get were lawn mowers, brushes made of hair or bristle, boxed candy, beer mugs, glass eyes (two thirds of which normally were imported from Germany), lobster forks and ice skates (Hollywood's highest-paid star, skater Sonja Henie, took out a $250,000 insurance policy on her last five pairs of skates). And alarm clocks were not available either until 1943, when complaints from factory managers about tardy employees forced the government to authorize production of a "Victory model" that economized on metal. From time to time, cigarettes virtually disappeared, and even when they were available smokers often had trouble finding book matches. Lucky Strike smokers had to get by without the familiar green package; because the ink contained precious metals, asserted the advertisements, "Lucky Strike green has gone to war." Skeptics contended the real reason was that the manufacturers of Lucky Strikes had been wanting to switch to a white package in order to attract more women smokers and had found a way to do it without offending their old customers.

One of the most important things that people had to do without was adequate housing. Washington, D.C., was so swollen with new government workers that apartment hunters were said to be committing mayhem to find lodg-

POINT BY POINT THROUGH THE MAZE OF RATIONING

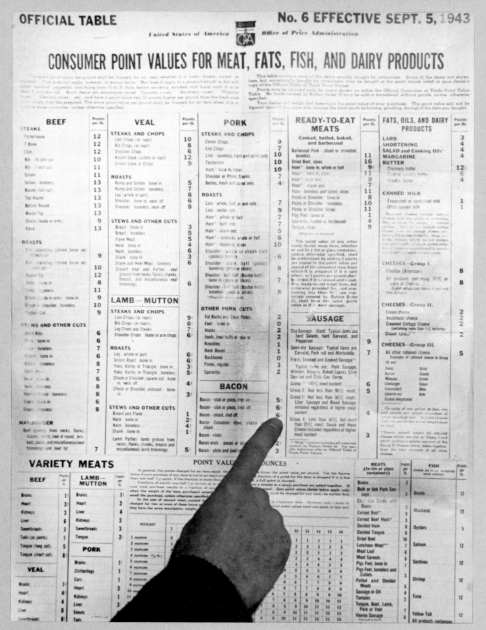

OFFICIAL TABLE — No. 6 EFFECTIVE SEPT. 5, 1943

United States of America — Office of Price Administration

CONSUMER POINT VALUES FOR MEAT, FATS, FISH, AND DAIRY PRODUCTS

An OPA agent puts a finger on the cost—in ration points—of a pound of bacon in September 1943. To help minimize confusion, the OPA periodically issued charts, as well as instruction booklets, that showed shoppers how to get the most out of ration coupons by judicious combination of points and foods.

Few wartime measures had so great an impact on the home front as food rationing. Sugar and coffee were the first items to be rationed, starting in 1942. The next year processed foods—soups, vegetables, canned juices—were added to the list, followed by meat, fish and dairy products. Shopping became a complicated and often frustrating experience.

Every individual was issued two ration books. One contained blue coupons for canned goods and the other was made up of red coupons for meat, fish and dairy products. Each person was allowed 48 blue points and 64 red points per month. A housewife shopping for canned goods for a family of four had a total of 192 points to use however she chose. At the start of a new month everyone got new ration stamps—and new sets of figures to juggle. Reflecting the availability of foods, applesauce took 10 points in March 1943 and climbed up to 25 in March a year later—while grapefruit juice dropped from 23 to four. The system created headaches for all —the Office of Price Administration (OPA) no less than the grocer, the butcher and their customers.

In a butcher-shop meat counter in March 1943, both prices and points are clearly marked.

At the canned-fruit shelves, a woman does some mental arithmetic, assessing the loss to her coupon book of 12 points for a 16-cent item.

Surveying the government's latest rationing regulations, a grocer scratches his head over the task of keeping his stock labeled correctly.

ing. A favorite story told by Henry F. Pringle, a writer who worked for the Office of War Information, described a man drowning in the Potomac River, whose cries for help attracted a passerby.

"What is your name and where do you live?" demanded the passerby.

"John Jones, 14 North S Street—Help!" the drowning man gasped frantically.

The passerby immediately rushed to that address and breathlessly told the landlady: "I want to rent John Jones's room. He just drowned."

"Sorry," replied the landlady, "it was just taken by the man who pushed him in."

Shortages had the effect of accelerating the search for substitutes and alternatives, some of which survived the War. Plastics replaced hard-to-get metals and rubber. The pocket-sized paperback books, which used far less paper and were easily mailable to servicemen overseas, gained a foothold in publishing. Margarine supplanted butter, although the vegetable matter that gave it its golden color had to be blended in by hand.

One substitute that did not endure was "Olde Spud," an ersatz whiskey made from alcohol distilled from waste potatoes. Alcohol was needed for explosives, and real whiskey disappeared just at a time when wartime jitters and booming wages had increased hard drinking by 30 per cent. "If people go into a store and can't buy butter," said a distillery executive, "they accept it because there's a war on. But if they can't get whiskey they raise hell."

For the most part, however, Americans made do with what they had and wore their little sacrifices like badges of honor. This was literally true in the case of shortage-induced changes in clothing fashions. Patched apparel, for example, became something of a fad, perhaps because it indicated a patriotic sacrifice. Men wore "Victory suits" that saved cloth because they came with only one pair of pants, narrow lapels, short jackets and no vests or cuffs. Women's skirts ended an inch above the knee—by OPA decree—and their swimming suits were two-piece, leading the staid *Wall Street Journal* to report: "The saving has been effected in the region of the midriff."

Women's legs also were bare. Even before the War, the silk ordinarily used for stockings had been diverted to mak-

ing parachutes. And after Pearl Harbor cut off the silk supply from Japan, the new synthetic nylon followed the same route. Women had to make do with leg make-up, the so-called "bottled stockings" that with luck and no baths, it was said, would last three days. Many women even artfully created the illusion of a seam down the back of the leg by applying a stripe with an eyebrow pencil. For men the principal problem with the leg make-up worn by women was the fact that, in the words of a popular song, "It decants on your pants."

Women's make-do spirit was dramatically symbolized in the wedding dress of Hollywood starlet Elyse Knox when

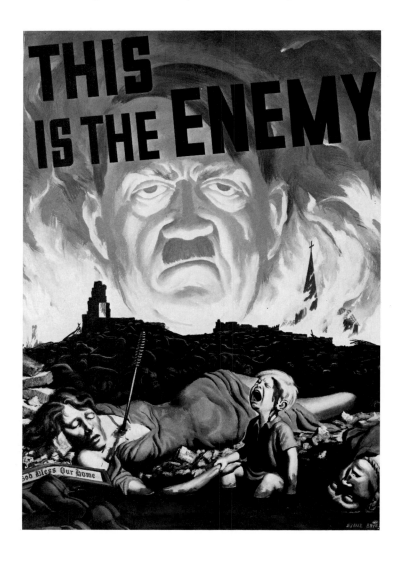

The grim visage of Adolf Hitler looms over a sea of carnage and burning buildings in this propaganda poster designed to fuel hatred for the enemy. It took top honors in a poster competition at New York's Museum of Modern Art in 1942. Many of the 200 entries were later distributed by the Office of War Information to U.S. factories and public buildings.

she married the flying hero and former football star Tommy Harmon. The bridegroom had bailed out twice from planes about to crash, and his bride's silk gown was fashioned from the remnants of one of his parachutes.

In addition to shortages of material goods, Americans had to accept some limits on freedom of expression. It became a familiar experience to receive a letter from a soldier or sailor overseas that had been slit open, a few words or sentences snipped out and then the envelope resealed with a bit of tape saying, "Opened by censor." Every bit of correspondence entering or leaving the United States was subject to censorship.

At the head of the newly formed Office of Censorship was a highly respected newsman, Byron Price, who had been general manager of the Associated Press. Price instituted a voluntary code for publishers and broadcasters. News of ship and troop movements and battle casualties was restricted. Such radio staples as man-on-the-street interviews and musical-request shows also were barred, on the ground that they could be exploited to transmit coded messages. As one government official suggested, " 'The Star-Spangled Banner' can be played in a manner to convey a message from someone in Kansas City to someone in Mexico." The Office of Censorship had a clearance desk that operated 24 hours a day so that editors in doubt about whether a story might damage the war effort could get an instant determination.

Editors and broadcasters occasionally defied the Office of Censorship. One newspaper, on learning that the Japanese balloon story was being spread by word of mouth through luncheon clubs and fraternal organizations, reported the existence of the deadly balloons to its readers. The editor contended that Japanese spies were not deaf, and if they were going to hear about the success of the balloon bombs they might as well read about it.

While officially suppressing news of the balloon bombs, the government gave wide publicity to the threat of domestically launched espionage—a policy that was intended both to protect the home front and to unite it. Slogans such as "Enemy agents are always near; if you don't talk they won't hear" appeared on the walls of munitions factories. Other posters warned people living in port cities that "A slip of the lip may sink a ship." Newspaper ads encouraged readers to cooperate "with the FBI in apprehending suspicious characters." Such characters might be enemy agents sneaked into the United States or the home-grown variety of saboteur known as the "fifth columnist." The phrase had originated during the Spanish Civil War when General Emilio Mola, closing in on Madrid with four columns of Nationalist soldiers, remarked that he had a fifth column of Nationalist sympathizers within the city.

Fears about a fifth column in the U.S. during World War II, however, proved largely groundless. All together, the FBI investigated 19,649 suspected cases of internal sabotage and could not find one that was enemy directed. Still, a daring sabotage attempt in mid-1942 demonstrated that—in the watchwords often repeated in those days—"it could happen here."

Just before dawn on June 13, the U-boat *Innsbruck* surfaced off Long Island, cruised to within 500 yards of the beach and put ashore four men in a large rubber raft. The four Germans all had lived in the U.S. before the War. They spoke English fluently, knew American customs and geography, and had been trained in a special school for saboteurs near Berlin. A similar team landed by submarine on the Florida coast four days later. The intended targets were aluminum plants, locks on the Ohio River and rail lines. Together the two teams had enough explosives and incendiaries to conduct a two-year campaign of havoc against American war production.

The deadly serious mission began to stumble, however, as soon as the first team hit the beach on Long Island. The saboteurs had landed half a mile from a Coast Guard station. As they were changing into civilian clothes on the beach, an unarmed Coastguardsman caught them with their pants down. Though the team leader pretended they were lost American fishermen and forced $300 on him to "have a good time and forget all about this," the Coastguardsman had heard one of the men speaking German. Well indoctrinated by home-front antisabotage propaganda, he returned with a search party, which found the explosives the saboteurs had hastily buried on the beach.

Meanwhile, the Germans had walked to the train station at Amagansett—blundering through a trailer camp on the way—and had taken the train to Manhattan. They bought clothes on Fifth Avenue, dined at Dinty Moore's restaurant and blabbed indiscreetly about their mission.

The leader of the Long Island team, George Dasch, an unstable and embittered naturalized American citizen, also did some talking to the FBI. Dasch had felt cheated for most of his life, and he thought that by telling all to the FBI he would be gratefully rewarded.

While all this was going on, the team that landed in Florida had split into two groups. One pair proceeded to New York by train, detouring through Cincinnati because they feared that the East Coast would be heavily guarded. The others went to Chicago to visit relatives and await further orders. Within two weeks of the Long Island landing, the FBI had rounded up both teams.

The eight saboteurs were tried immediately before a military commission in almost total secrecy. All of the men were sentenced to death, but President Roosevelt commuted to 30 years in prison the sentences of Dasch and another saboteur who had defected with him. The two were released after serving five years. The other six were electrocuted, and Roosevelt's only regret, he would say later, was that they were not hanged—a punishment he considered more fitting for their attempted crimes.

Concurrent with the government's attempt to prevent damaging leaks to the enemy through censorship was a major effort to whip the people up to a fever pitch of hatred for the Germans and the Japanese. Emotions were skillfully stirred up in magazine articles such as "We Shall Hate or We Shall Fail," written by the mystery novelist Rex Stout, chairman of the government-affiliated Writers War Board, which enrolled some 2,000 writers in the American war effort. Stout's animosity was aimed at the German people, though most Americans considered Hitler, rather than his people, the real enemy.

Hatred of the Japanese tended to blur the distinction between the people and their leaders and often appeared to be racially motivated. A government-approved ad in *The New York Times* showed a sinister Japanese face under the headline "RAT POISON WANTED." The caption said, "There's only one way to exterminate the slant-eyes—with gunpowder!" In fact, 13 per cent of the Americans questioned by public-opinion polls in 1944—fueled no doubt by stories of atrocities that were committed against the prisoners of war and civilians in occupied lands—favored "exterminating" every Japanese after the War was over.

At the same time, solidarity with the Allies was highly valued, reaching such absurd heights as *Gourmet* magazine's plea to its readers to help out the Chinese by buying almond cookies. The Chinese, like the British, were old friends of America, of course, but the ground swell of admiration for the Russian dictator Josef Stalin and the Soviet Union was something else. The World War I air ace Captain Eddie Rickenbacker, a staunch conservative, came back from a tour of the Soviet Union in 1943 impressed by the iron discipline in its factories and the lack of "labor difficulties." And in the early part of 1942, at the 51st Continental Congress of the Daughters of the American Revolution, Mrs. Tryphosa Duncan Bates-Batcheller myopically informed her sisters: "Today in Russia, Communism is practically nonexistent."

If, by chance, Americans momentarily forgot there was a war on, they were quickly jolted back to reality by an assault of slogans, movies, songs and symbols. "Pay Your Taxes, Beat the Axis," proclaimed billboards and posters. Hollywood was advised by the government's Bureau of Motion Pictures that before undertaking a new movie, directors should ask themselves, "Will this picture help win the War?" The search for songs to help win the War led to so many abominations—among them, "The Japs Don't Have a Chinaman's Chance" and "We're Gonna Find a Feller Who Is Yeller and Beat Him Red, White and Blue"—that Representative J. Parnell Thomas of Pennsylvania lamented: "What this country needs is a good five-cent war song—something with plenty of zip, ginger and fire." The song that came closest to that prescription was "Praise the

Lord and Pass the Ammunition" by Frank Loesser, who based it loosely on the exploits of a chaplain at Pearl Harbor. Another that won popularity, "Coming In on a Wing and a Prayer," described the emergency landing of a damaged plane.

For long-lasting dramatic impact, however, no song or phrase could match that universal symbol of the American and Allied cause—V for Victory. It had been launched in 1940 by a Belgian refugee named Victor de Laveleye, who made daily short-wave broadcasts to his occupied country from London. He suggested that Belgians chalk the letter V for *Victoire* in public places to show their defiance of the German occupation. Because of its versatility—in Dutch, V stood for *Vrÿheid* (freedom), in Serbian for *Viteštvo* (heroism) and in Czech for *Vítězství* (victory)—the symbol quickly proliferated throughout Nazi-held Europe. Occupied peoples tapped out its Morse-code equivalent by knocking on doors, honking car horns and even tooting train whistles.

In the U.S., the V symbol appeared in such various forms as a $5,000 diamond brooch at Tiffany's and a lighting display at Louisiana State University in which red, white and blue bulbs flashed in the three-dots-and-a-dash rhythm. That rhythm also had powerful echoes in the first four notes of Beethoven's Fifth Symphony. For that reason, in 1943 when Arturo Toscanini conducted the NBC Symphony Orchestra in a special concert that was broadcast both in the U.S. and to his native Italy, he chose to lead off with the first movement of Beethoven's Fifth. In an earlier protest against fascism, Toscanini had resigned as director of Milan's La Scala Opera House; before leaving Italy he had been beaten by Mussolini's police. Now, as the 76-year-old maestro conducted the familiar opening notes, "dit-dit-dit-dah," tears streamed down his face. The concert was so enormously popular that NBC rebroadcast it repeatedly.

The manipulation of symbols and words—propaganda—was the primary function of the Office of War Information, which was headed by Elmer Davis, a former network newscaster whose Indiana twang was familiar to millions. In addition to coordinating the dissemination of war information, the OWI was responsible for explaining, at home and abroad, U.S. policies and aims. The latter function finally resulted in a major split in the agency. On the one side were writers and intellectuals—among them, the young historian Arthur Schlesinger Jr.—who felt that the War's deeper issues were not being adequately spelled out to the American people. (In March 1942, for example, a majority of those polled admitted having no "clear idea of what the War is all about.") The writers wanted to stress the need to extinguish fascism and to achieve the Four Freedoms proclaimed by President Roosevelt: freedom of expression, freedom of religion, freedom from want and freedom from fear. On the other side were the advertising men recruited from Madison Avenue, who—the writers asserted—preferred "slick salesmanship to honest information."

In the spring of 1943, fifteen of the writers resigned, angrily accusing the OWI of attempting "to soft-soap the American public." To dramatize the charge, one of the writers created a mock poster that satirized both the Madison Avenue approach and the dissidents' allegiance to the lofty war principles enunciated by President Roosevelt. The poster, showing the Statue of Liberty holding aloft a frosty bottle of Coca-Cola instead of the torch, was captioned: "Try the Four Delicious Freedoms—the War that Refreshes."

The fact was that, in a manner the writer had not intended, the War *was* a refreshing experience for many people on the home front. Sociologists reported finding a widespread sense of "unconscious well-being," which they attributed to participation in civilian defense, scrap drives and the other efforts to bring the War home. Moreover, compared with the British, the Russians, the Germans and the Japanese, Americans were fortunate indeed. A poll taken midway through the War made clear that despite the shortages and the rationing, few on the home front harbored illusions about the caliber of hardships they were enduring: nearly seven in 10 readily admitted that the War had not demanded of them "any real sacrifices."

THE YOUNGEST WARRIORS

Youngsters in Roanoke, Virginia, their pony cart laden with discarded toys, housewares and other junk, add to their day's collection during a scrap-metal drive.

BASIC TRAINING AT AN EARLY AGE

Armed with wooden guns and wearing tin helmets, three boys scale a barrier in a Junior Commando drill at the Detroit Boys Club playground.

Even though they were thousands of miles from the bombings and the battlefields, America's children were indelibly touched by the War. They grew up in a war atmosphere, where frequently their fathers were known to them only as pictures on bureaus and their mothers were away for long stretches, working in defense plants or on other war-related jobs. They played war games and felt the effect of shortages, as rubber balls, tricycles and doll carriages—all made of critical war materials—disappeared for the duration.

The youngsters pitched in with gusto to help with the war effort. They made clothes for children in war-devastated lands and knitted socks for GIs overseas. Some of them collected milkweed pods, whose fluffy insides were used to fill life jackets. Others packed flour-filled "bombs" for mock air raids in civilian-defense exercises.

In classrooms throughout the country, children plunked down oceans of nickels and dimes for War Stamps and Bonds. In 1944 alone, school sales of bonds and stamps purchased 11,700 parachutes, 2,900 planes and more than 44,000 jeeps for America's armed forces.

The same enthusiasm prevailed in scrap drives, as legions of small fry picked their neighborhoods clean of paper, scrap metal, tin foil and old tires for war production. In Chicago, thousands of children took to the streets and in five months' time collected 18,000 tons of newspaper.

Most of these activities were channeled through schools and youth organizations, like the Junior Service Corps, the Junior Red Cross, 4-H Clubs, the Boy Scouts and Girl Scouts. Taking a cue from the comic-strip character Little Orphan Annie, the children also joined an organization called Junior Commandos, which was modeled after the Army with captains, majors and colonels. The commandos collected scrap, played war games, and huffed and puffed their way over rugged obstacle courses *(left)*.

Along with other children, they enlisted for the duration. While many adults quickly lost their enthusiasm for scrap drives and other war activities, the youngsters never let up until the War was over.

West Coast youngsters, pretending to stave off a Japanese invasion, crouch behind a dirt embankment next to an American soldier on guard against the real thing.

A group of New York City school children line up in their classroom to buy War Stamps from a School Defense Aid volunteer. The SDA volunteers, mothers of the youngsters, also supervised air-raid drills held in the schools.

A young artist in a San Leandro, California, schoolroom sketches an American bombing raid on the blackboard to promote the sale of War Bonds to his classmates. During the War, U.S. school children accounted for more than a billion dollars' worth of stamps and bonds.

In a practice drill, children of Friends Seminary, one of New York's oldest schools, huddle with their teachers in the hallway of a fireproof building that served as an air-raid shelter.

Using utensils as helmets, boys from the Grand Street Settlement in New York noisily exhort residents on the Lower East Side to contribute aluminum for scrap.

New York Junior Commandos inventory their day's take of scrap paper. The bemedaled youngster at right is a colonel, the other boys are majors.

Junior Commandos in Roanoke wait patiently to turn in their weekly collection of fats and greases, which yielded glycerin for high explosives.

Boy Scouts lead a parade of trucks, carrying more than 80 tons of old automobile and bicycle tires, through Stevens Point, Wisconsin, in June 1942. When Japanese conquests in the Far East cut off almost all of the United States' natural rubber supply, President Roosevelt called for a nationwide scrap drive. Responding to the appeal, Scouts across the country collected more than 54,000 tons of rubber.

ONE FAMILY'S WAR

The family of Albert and Louise Wood relaxes after tennis at the home of a neighbor in 1939, when the prospect of war still seemed remote to most Americans.

THE LONELINESS OF THOSE LEFT BEHIND

On Christmas Eve, 1944, Albert and Louise Wood of Port Washington, New York, lighted a large green candle and placed it in the center of their dining-room table. They had written to their four sons serving in uniform at widely scattered posts around the globe that they would keep the candle burning for 30 hours, and by remembering its flame the family would be together, at least in spirit, on Christmas Day. The candlelighting was one small ceremonial in what had become for the Wood parents an unspoken vigil against the festive day when their sons would come home from the War. So it was all over America: families endured the interminable wait, yearning for good news, dreading the bad, sharing a common anxiety and sometimes a common grief.

Before the War intruded, the prodigious Wood family—five sons and two daughters—was an inseparable clan living together in the same house, working together as cabinet-makers in the family business that bore the proud name Albert Wood & Five Sons. "We were the closest family you could imagine," Mari, one of the daughters, later recalled. "We were creating beautiful pieces of furniture that were works of art. We gathered every day for meals, and our dinners lasted two hours and were full of long conversations and laughter. But because there were five boys, the War was hanging over us."

One by one, the Woods' sons were inducted until finally only the oldest remained. The big house at 19 Second Avenue was unnaturally quiet, the evenings long and lonely in the absence of the young men. Albert Wood converted the furniture shop for production of aircraft parts—high-priority war work for which the oldest son was exempted from service. Then, on the night of January 19, 1945, Albert and Louise Wood heard a knock at the door. A messenger had arrived with a War Department telegram. "REGRET TO INFORM YOU YOUR SON STAFF SERGEANT FRANCIS F WOOD SERIOUSLY WOUNDED IN ACTION," it began, in the terse phrases so familiar to countless Americans. In that moment the War came home to the Wood family with a force that only those most deeply involved could ever know.

Beneath the sign of the family business, the five Wood brothers—from the left, Francis, Gardner, Bertram, Paul and Moyer—strike a fraternal pose.

While her sons are away in uniform, Louise Wood maintains her daily watch for the postman through the dining-room window of her Long Island home.

Albert Wood, an architect and designer, works at his drafting table at home at a time when only one son remained in Port Washington to help with the family cabinetmaking business.

ECHOES OF LAUGHTER IN A HALF-EMPTY HOUSE

For those who were left behind during the War, the only answer to the loneliness and the anxiety was to keep as busy as possible. Albert Wood steeped himself in work as a defense contractor to block what he called "the thoughts of total disaster which occasionally flitted through my mind." Louise Wood kept the overseas mailbags heavy with cookies for her sons. She filled her newsletter, "The Buzzer," with news of other family members and details of the home life that the boys had left behind. And she kept the daily and sometimes disappointing watch for their replies.

When they were not at work, Albert and Louise turned to their favorite hobbies to pass the time. "Revivals are the rage at 19 Second Avenue," Louise noted in "The Buzzer" in January 1945. "The cribbage board was dusted off, and now Louise and Albert play three or four nights a week. New strings were put on Albert's neglected violin and he came home with a pile of new music. Great aides to our morale."

Sitting alone on the steps of her sunny front porch, Louise Wood reads a paper to keep up with news of the War that took her sons.

Facing a portrait of her son Gardner in his Army Air Forces uniform, Louise plays the piano. She preferred lively Chopin waltzes and her favorite hymns when she needed cheering up.

At home on leave after completing his basic training, Paul, the youngest son, strolls with his mother around a neighbor's lawn.

Mari Wood proudly displays her Red Cross uniform. She volunteered in 1942; later, she toured Europe as an actress with the USO.

With his daughter Anne as a passenger, Moyer Wood, the oldest son, sets out for work at the family shop in downtown Port Washington.

Flanked by his daughters, Penelope (right) and Mari, Albert Wood celebrates his 59th birthday in 1945 with a quiet champagne party.

Standing beside the family car, Gardner, on leave from the Army Air Forces, chats with his brothers and sisters before going to visit friends.

THE FLEETING JOYS OF BRIEF REUNIONS

"Sunday evening, about seven o'clock, the front door opened violently, a uniformed six-footer tore up the stairs and burst into the living room and into the arms of—his Mama!" This entry in the family newsletter by Louise Wood indicates the unrestrained joy that accompanied the furloughs of her sons; on such occasions, the remnants of the clan gathered, the talk began, the tension and loneliness of waiting eased.

But such holidays were rare, and during the long periods of time in between, Louise's preoccupation with her absent sons frequently made it difficult for her to concentrate on anything else. Once, she began hand-vacuuming a rug, only to discover that she was pushing a toaster across the floor. She and her husband determined to take a memory-sharpening course to combat an increasing absent-mindedness.

Both aged visibly; everything seemed to remind them of the War. Writing about a trip to the seashore, Louise noted: "The War has touched Jones Beach, too. The crowd was small and quiet, and even the surf seemed subdued."

Penelope Wood (center foreground), the youngest member of the family, assists some of her classmates at Manhasset Bay School in laying out rows for a Victory garden.

In training in Louisiana, Bertram, an Army private, stages a theatrical leap for a snapshot he sent home.

Francis manages a smile during basic training.

KEEPING THE FAMILY TOGETHER

For more than three years during the War the family ties among the Woods were maintained by reams of letters, telegrams and the monthly editions of "The Buzzer," the newsletter edited by Louise. All of these communications were boundlessly optimistic and filled with affection. In the letters the sons sent home, there were echoes of the happy life the family had enjoyed in Port Washington before the War. Francis wrote his parents of a French family that housed him: "A wife who takes pride in preparing something well, a husband who is a fine host. A considerate, generous family. Everything that you and Mom have always practiced and shown."

Gardner, a staff sergeant in the spring of 1944, strikes a pensive pose at his Orlando, Florida, air base.

Paul projects nonchalance in his Army khakis.

Number VII   Vol. 1
ARMISTICE DAY: November 11, 1944.   Weather: Balmy

THE BUZZER

"Buzz, buzz, buzz goes the Buzzer!"

One day, all fear, all ugliness,
All pain, all discord, dumb or loud,
All selfishness, and all distress
Will melt like low-spread morning cloud,
And heart and brain be free from thrall
Because Thou, God, art all in all.

                                    - George Macdonald

FRANCIS RECEIVES HIS FIRST LETTER FROM HOME!   ALSO
HIS FIRST LETTER FROM BIRDIE IN HOLLAND.

S/SGT. GARDNER TRANSFERRED FROM THE ARMY TO THE NACA -
NATIONAL ADVISORY COMMITTEE OF AERONAUTICS.   NOW A
CIVILIAN HIS NEW STATION IS LANGLEY FIELD VIRGINIA

PFC. PAUL ARRIVES HOME FROM CALIFORNIA FOR A THIRTEEN
DAY FURLOUGH

MOYER AND BETTY WOOD BUY A FORD CAR   (See story page 4)

TOM MORGAN PRESIDENT SPERRY CORPORATION SPENDS TWO
HOURS IN THE SHOPS OF ALBERT WOOD & FIVE SONS

THE FOUNDER OF THE FIRM is continually surprising and
delighting his family.   No sooner was the drafting room completed
than he undertook a commission for Tom Morgan, head of the Sperry
Corporation. Moyer was completely tied up with contracts for the
Sperry Gyroscope Company, so to relieve him of concern for this
new work, Albert took it on. He made a beautiful design, approved
immediately by Mr. Morgan, for the experimental case which was to
house an experimental radio receiving and broadcasting set with
Capeheart Record changer, etc., on which Sperry Experimental
Laboratory had been working for six months. The final result, with
which Mr. Morgan is tremendously pleased, is a knockout. The first
beautifully designed radio cabinet in existence. The unique sliding
doors a triumph of workmanship!

THE LITTLE CORPORAL WHOSE ACTIVITIES are now confined to the
Cheese Country writes that he has become a cheese addict, that it
has become a necessary part of his daily diet. Will wonders never
cease! Francis admits that he, in turn, has grown insanely fond of
coffee. AND American cheese!

Mari and Bob love Philadelphia. Mari must have fifteen
thousand fifth cousins living in the City of Brotherly Love.

Louise Wood headlined the activities of the various members of her family on the title page of her newsletter, then gave fuller details inside. "The Buzzer" usually ran four pages.

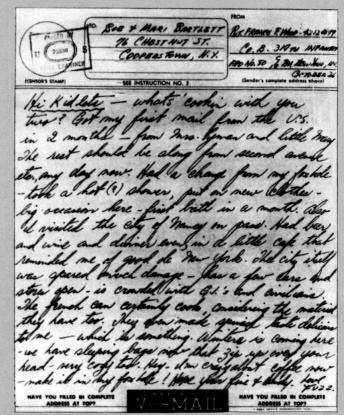

In a cheerful V-Mail letter to his sister Mari and her husband, Bob, then in Cooperstown, New York, Francis describes a pleasant break for a frontline soldier. Two months later he was wounded.

Paul, whose nickname was "Pill," wrote from Hawaii to his sister Mari, using his pet name for her, "Sete." The letter was censored to delete the mention of a date and a wounded friend.

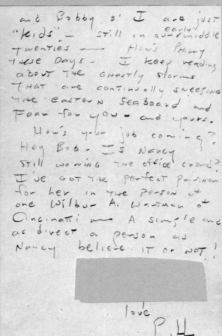

AN OMINOUS MESSAGE FROM WASHINGTON

"I'm sorry to be the one to deliver this," the taxi driver said to Albert Wood as he handed him the envelope. The message would make January 19, 1945, the darkest day of the War for the Woods. Albert later recalled: "I realized the driver knew the contents of my telegram, and that it must be one of those next-of-kin missives I'd hoped never to receive." The message was blunt. Francis had been seriously wounded in the Battle of the Bulge.

After several weeks with practically no news of their son's condition, Albert and Louise were relieved to learn from a friend who visited Francis at a hospital in England that he was recovering nicely. "The war in the Pacific was not over, and we began to feel anxious about Paul," Albert wrote, his words hinting of the ordeal that faced parents with sons still fighting.

Francis Wood was twice wounded and received the Purple Heart with oak leaf cluster (right). The first wound was minor; the second one was revealed to his parents in this telegram.

Relaxing in Bavaria, where he was stationed in the late summer of 1945, Francis enjoys a liqueur that he once described as "sweet and powerful as this new atomic bomb."

Francis sent his parents a photograph (above) of his scar. Five weeks after his family learned of his injury, the Army mailed them an abruptly worded bulletin (below) on his progress.

Louise and Albert played together often in the winter of 1945. After their son Francis was wounded and news was scarce, they turned to music for solace.

Home from the War, the Wood clan celebrates in Port Washington. In the foreground are Francis (left) and Bertram. Standing (from left) are: Moyer, brother-in-law Robert Bartlett, Penelope, Albert and Gardner.

The patriarch of the family and his wife, Louise, host a postwar gathering for some of the children and their wives, husbands and girl friends in the elegant dining room of the Waldorf Astoria Hotel in New York City.

SONS REUNITED AFTER THE TEST OF FIRE

The sons of Albert and Louise Wood returned from the War eager to make up the time that they had sacrificed. Only Francis bore a scar, but all four had changed. Like so many fathers of his generation, Albert Wood discovered that his sons had left home as boys and had been forged by the fires of their experience into men. At first he found it difficult to adjust to their sudden maturity, their new sense of independence and their reluctance to resume life exactly as it had been before the War. But he came to accept these changes. "We all polished up our rose-colored glasses," Albert said of this period, "and peered deeper into what we thought the world of everlasting peace held in store for us."

His sons had always been artistically inclined, and now they plunged into the arts: acting, writing, painting and sculpture. But gradually, as the last of their Army paychecks diminished, they began to spend more time in the shop of Albert Wood & Five Sons, finding again the old pleasure of working together in Port Washington—and looking ahead to the future.

5

Sometime during the autumn of 1942 an Iowan named John R. Brauckmiller decided to pull up stakes and go West. Like thousands of Americans seized with the same notion, he had motives both patriotic and personal. By getting a job in some shipyard along the booming Pacific Coast, he would not only be doing his bit for the war effort but also bettering the income he had been able to earn as a construction worker and blacksmith in Grand Island, Nebraska.

Brauckmiller, however, was not exactly foot-loose. He had a wife, 10 sons, three daughters and 16 grandchildren. Although several had left the fold—one son to go into the Army, another to work in a defense plant in the East, a daughter to live near the Army camp where her husband was stationed—the rest of the Brauckmillers were still close-knit. They saw no reason to disrupt their happy state. And so they migrated en masse, traveling in assorted jalopies and arriving at their chosen destination—Portland, Oregon—in successive waves.

The trek failed to dampen the Brauckmillers' zest for togetherness. Before long, 15 of them had found jobs at the same place—Henry J. Kaiser's Swan Island shipyard—and on the same midnight-to-morning graveyard shift. Grandpa Brauckmiller, eight sons and a son-in-law worked as shipfitters, while a daughter and four daughters-in-law worked as welders, welder's helpers and shipfitter's helpers. Grandma Brauckmiller might have joined them except that she was keeping house, looking after her youngest daughter and grandchildren, tending the family pooch and canary, feeding three non-Brauckmiller boarders and, as a sideline, renting out two furnished rooms to transients. Portland, like other cities that were reaping a bonanza in war contracts, was crowded and short of housing; Grandma, after a lifetime of enforced frugality, was not about to miss a chance at some extra cash.

But the Brauckmillers' lean years were over. The shipyard contingent's combined weekly take at the Kaiser pay windows averaged a princely $996. Even after it was split among the 15 individual earners, the pay was enough to permit them to invest anywhere from a tenth to a half of their wages in War Bonds.

Numerous though they may have been, the Brauckmillers were by no means unique in pulling up stakes. They were part of a mass movement that was one of the home front's

A NATION IN MOTION

most dramatic features. America was a nation in motion during the War. An estimated 40 million people left home, and not just for training camps or assignments overseas, but to find jobs or seek their fortunes in other parts of the country. Moreover, the dislocation was not just physical, but social and psychological as well. By providing rich new job opportunities and putting rivers of money into circulation, the War produced sudden and startling changes in the economic and social status of many people. In the process, it subjected individuals, families and the whole fabric of American society to great strains.

In addition to the 16 million people who left home for military service, an estimated 15.3 million civilians changed their residences across county lines. For most of them the magnet was jobs, often in places far from where they had been living. According to Bureau of Census estimates, 7.7 million Americans moved to other states and 3.6 million to different parts of the country. California's shipyards and aircraft plants alone attracted 1.4 million people, helping to set the stage for the state's later ascendancy as the largest population center in the United States.

As an early result of the massive reshuffling of the population, acute shortages of housing developed. Hundreds of boomtowns appeared across the nation, as the sheer numbers of new migrants quickly overwhelmed existing housing, schools and other facilities. Around many cities instant slums sprang up—so-called "new Hoovervilles" that consisted of trailer camps, shantytowns and tent settlements. A sense of impermanence governed the lives of many of the newcomers, and the established residents did little to ease their plight. "Those folks in houses think trailer people are vermin," a newcomer to Pascagoula, Mississippi, told reporter Agnes E. Meyer, whose investigations of boomtowns were later published in a book aptly titled *Journey through Chaos.*

No other area of the country felt the effects of the migration more sharply than the South. The boom came early there—before Pearl Harbor—raising the entire region up from the economic stagnation that had beset it since the Civil War. Its resurgence stemmed in part from the scores of military training camps located there. Starke, Florida, formerly a depressed backwater town with a population of 1,500, overnight became the state's fourth largest city when

Camp Blanding, a post for 60,000 soldiers, was built close by. More than 20,000 men were employed in its construction; local accommodations were inundated, and residents were persuaded to open their homes to those in need of shelter. Still, some who were unable to find other housing slept in cars or lived in lean-tos, roadside brush piles or even packing cases.

Many Southern cities, converting in a hurry to heavy industrialization, were overrun by newly arriving workers. The situation was most acute along the Gulf Coast, where shipyards drew tens of thousands of job seekers from the backwoods. In Mobile, Alabama, the population shot up 60 per cent in three years. So crowded was the metropolitan area that landlords rented so-called "hot beds" to workers in shifts—eight hours' rest for 25 cents. To the visiting author John Dos Passos, Mobile looked "trampled and battered like a city that's been taken by storm." He noted, however, that the living conditions there, though primitive, were often an improvement over the new residents' previous lot: "Housekeeping in a trailer with electric light and running water is a dazzling luxury to a woman who's lived all her life in a cabin with half-inch chinks between the splintered boards of the floor."

The lack of housing was critical elsewhere, too: in Portland, where the Brauckmillers settled; in Hartford, Connecticut, and San Diego, California, where many workers lived in barely furnished rooms, makeshift houses and trailer camps that the head of the Federal Security Administration said constituted a new kind of "slum on wheels." The most notorious boomtown was Willow Run, Michigan, site of the giant Ford aircraft plant. The plant attracted more than 32,000 new residents to the area, and its assembly-line technology contrasted cruelly with the primitive living conditions around it. Outdoor privies were situated dangerously near wells. One fairly typical house served five men living in the basement, a family of five on the first floor, four people on the second floor, nine men in the garage and four families in four trailers parked in the yard. Working in the Ford plant was not so bad, a resident told a visiting reporter, but after being cooped up in the trailers all day the women went "trailerwacky."

To alleviate the housing shortage at Willow Run, the federal government planned construction of a permanent community that was to accommodate 30,000 people. But the plan ran into heavy opposition. Residents of the area opposed permanent housing because they feared that Willow Run would become a ghost town and tax burden after the War. And Ford officials feared that the existence of a permanent community would strengthen the auto workers' union. When surveyors began work on the project, Ford security men ripped up the surveying stakes. Eventually 10,000 temporary housing units were constructed, half in the form of dormitories for single men and women.

As America's war plants went into full production, the country became prosperous once more. Unemployment levels and the number of low-paying jobs declined dramati-

Dubbed by a West Coast newspaper as "the shipbuildingest family in America," the hard-hatted clan of John R. Brauckmiller (sixth from left) perches on a railing at Portland, Oregon's Swan Island shipyard. There, 15 Brauckmiller kin found jobs after migrating en masse from the Midwest in search of a larger share of America's generous wartime wages.

cally. Overall, personal income soared from $96 billion to $171 billion in the four War years. The weekly earnings of the average factory worker nearly doubled, rising from $25.25 to $47.08, and many people (such as the Brauckmillers) did much better. With the economy running at top speed, some workers began to eye the prospect of peace with ambivalence. "It's a pretty good war if you don't get shot at," one man said.

After stinting through a decade of Depression, people suddenly had money to spend, and they did not let rationing or shortages stop them from doing so. Production of consumer goods rose by 12 per cent in spite of the high priority accorded war materials, and the nation went on a spending spree. "People are crazy with money," observed a jeweler in Philadelphia. "They don't care what they buy." They bought furs, cosmetics, handbags. Jewelry sales rose 26 per cent in 1942. On the third anniversary of Pearl Harbor, Macy's department store in New York City enjoyed a record-breaking selling day.

Driven by the pressures and tensions brought on by the War, people began to spend lavishly on entertainment. Wartime business was up 40 per cent at nightclubs like New York's Latin Quarter, which featured elaborate, flashy shows. Lou Walters, the club's owner, explained: "You gotta keep in mind you are selling them luxury and waste." Broadway enjoyed its most prosperous season in 1944-1945, mainly with frothy, escapist fare. The movie business was also booming. In Portland, Oregon, theaters stayed open all night, featuring a workers' "swing-shift matinee" from midnight to 4 o'clock in the morning. Betting and attendance at race tracks reached their highest wartime levels in 1944 and 1945. "America was on the damndest gambling binge in its history," noted columnist Dan Parker of the New York *Daily News.*

To many soldiers returning to the United States from overseas, it often seemed that Americans at home were oblivious to the true dimensions of the War. "Their way of life hasn't really changed a damn bit," grumbled an Army Air Forces bombardier on furlough. His bitterness was understandable: civilians all around him appeared to be having the time of their lives. But in spite of the fun, economic and social changes of profound significance were taking place.

And in the process America was being irrevocably altered.

The new job opportunities and the new prosperity were the catalysts. Job prospects improved up and down the line. A poll showed that seven out of every 10 citizens questioned felt that they now had a better chance of getting ahead than their parents had possessed. Businessmen, farmers, women, skilled workers, unskilled workers shared in the good times. But the biggest gains came at the bottom of the social pyramid. While income in the top fifth increased by 20 per cent, it rose in the bottom fifth by 68 per cent. Perhaps the best index of the economic gains was the increase in the number of Americans who had to pay income taxes. In 1940, only 7.8 million filed tax returns; in 1945, no fewer than 48 million in a population of 140 million filed returns with the Internal Revenue Service. (To some degree the tax-paying population was increased as well by a reduction in the minimum taxable income from $800 to $500.)

The War was not only putting more money in most people's hands; it was having a democratizing effect as well through the impact of rationing and shortages. A social reformer pointed the fact out early in the War: "Rockefeller and I can now get the same amount of sugar, gasoline, tires, etc., etc., etc., and the etc.'s will soon fill many pages."

The gasoline shortage even forced that arbiter of upperclass manners, Emily Post, to revise her code. Hosts were no longer expected to pick up their guests at the train station, she ruled.

A more serious consequence for the upper crust was the fact that many lost their servants to the lure of wartime wages, never to get them back again. By 1944 the number of women in domestic work had decreased by one fifth. Newspaper want ads attested to the shortage of maids. A woman in Newark offered "room, radio, good salary and nice home," then desperately threw in the privilege of wearing her mink coat on days off.

The old ways died hard, of course, and the people who were high on the status ladder went to great lengths to maintain a semblance of social stratification. At a shipyard in Seneca, Illinois (which had direct access to the Mississippi River), the units of a new government-constructed housing project were all exactly alike—in style, quality and rent. But the shipyard quietly arranged for its executives to reside in

MAKING DO WITH TEEN-AGE POWER

With the War's growing appetite for able-bodied men consuming America's labor supply in the early 1940s, teen-age boys and girls were among those who filled in as replacements. At the same time, many states had to relax their child-labor laws to allow minors to work. By 1943, there were almost three million American boys and girls on the job in American fields and factories, half a million of them in defense plants where they were paid at the standard rate.

These striplings were not just poor substitutes for strong men; they pulled their share of the load, despite their lack of seasoning. One defense contractor, Lockheed Aircraft, hired 1,500 boys in 1943 as riveters, draftsmen, electricians and sheet-metal workers. Their delighted supervisors discovered that two young people working a four-hour shift accomplished more than an adult employee who was doing a regular eight-hour stint.

In the process of bringing great numbers of children into the work force, the War altered the lives of many adolescents. Lured by high wartime wages, they took jobs and forgot about their education. Between 1940 and 1944, the number of teen-age workers in America increased by 1.9 million; the number attending school declined by 1.25 million. Many who tried to combine school and work fell asleep in class, weary from the demands of the job.

In a California shipyard, Tom Powell (above right, foreground), 17, and his youthful co-workers chip excess metal from a jig used in the construction of ships. Roy Popp (right), 16, works on a transport plane's fuselage on the assembly line of a West Coast aircraft plant.

the block of houses nearest town. Although a carbon copy of all the others in the project, this block became known as "Gold Coast Row."

While people were growing richer, the physical and social upheavals of the War imposed severe strains on many of the country's most basic institutions. Foremost among these were marriage and the family, which endured conflicting and often intolerable stresses. The War had a double-edged effect. On the one hand the rash of whirlwind romances produced an upsurge of weddings and a startling rise in the birth rate. In 1943, after declining since the 1920s, the birth rate reached its highest level in two decades, thanks in no small part to the boom in "goodbye babies," those conceived just before their GI fathers left for overseas. At the same time, the divorce rate rose dramatically. In 1945 more than half a million marriages were dissolved—almost double the prewar figure.

The primary reason for the sharp increase in the number of divorces was, of course, the burden of long separation between servicemen and their wives. The women had to learn to wait; as one wife put it, "to endure the slow trickle of time from hour to hour, from day to day, for weeks in anguish and suspense." Some women sleepwalked through the War. Others cracked up or turned to alcohol for solace—by 1943 the ratio of female alcoholics to male had jumped from 1 to 5 to 1 to 2.

Infidelity, whether it was real or only imagined, was a principal source of stress for husbands and wives. A poll taken of young women in 1943 revealed that nearly half believed that their husbands were being untrue to them. Servicemen were equally worried about receiving "Dear John" letters from home, informing them that their wives or sweethearts had taken up with other men. Valid statistics on infidelity were not compiled during the pre-Kinsey era. But it was common enough across the Atlantic for a British bishop to suggest that at the end of the War all reunited couples should forgive each other's lapses and go through a second marriage ceremony in order to achieve a fresh start. A less conciliatory opinion was heard from the judge in New Jersey who declared, "If I had my way, soldiers' wives who are unfaithful would be branded with scarlet letters and have their heads shaven." The judge—who was a

man, of course—did not comment on unfaithful soldiers.

Problems of separation and infidelity had always plagued marriages in wartime, but World War II introduced a complicating factor. Many GIs came home to find that their wives had become much more independent. The new self-sufficiency stemmed from the fact that more than six million women, better than half of them married, had experienced for the first time the excitement and independence of earning their own paychecks (pages 88-101). For them divorce, or the prospect of living alone, lost some of its terror. In Iowa, sociologists studied 135 women whose husbands had gone to war. A sizable number of the wives "did not miss their husbands at all," the sociologists concluded and, indeed, "were glad to be free."

While the role of wife and mother was changing, the dislocations of the War were radically altering the status of another member of the family. This was the teenager, who acquired a new independence through the breakdown of normal family life and the availability of jobs that paid well. Aided by ready access to plenty of easy money and the relaxation of social constraints, the wartime crop of teenagers developed into a highly specialized subculture, with its own clothing styles, interests and problems. The young people evolved a dance known as the jitterbug, which required such strenuous hopping and leaping about that scarcely anyone over 20 could, in the teen-age parlance of the day, "cut a rug." Psychologists concluded that the jitterbug was—as one put it—"a mating dance that emulated sexual foreplay."

The psychologists also had a ready explanation for the teenagers' biggest craze—singer Frank Sinatra. They attributed his great appeal to frustrated love induced by the pressures of wartime. Whatever the cause, American show business had never before seen anything like the hysteria that surrounded this scrawny young man from Hoboken who was classified 4-F because of a punctured eardrum and whose voice reminded one adult critic of "worn velveteen." Teen-age girls swooned. Two girls almost strangled him in a tug of war with his bow tie. Once, when he sang "I'll Walk Alone," a voice from the audience cried out in Brooklynese: "I'll walk wid ya, Frankie." His appearance at Manhattan's Paramount Theater in 1944 caused a near riot by 30,000 teen-age girls (they were called "bobby-soxers"), and more than 700 policemen had to be called in to restore order.

Sinatra was blamed for teen-age truancy and was even denounced in Congress as one of "the prime instigators of juvenile delinquency in America." But other—and disparate—wartime phenomena were also blamed: working mothers, the absence of fathers, the sense of impermanence engendered by wartime mobility, the lack of customary social restraints in boomtowns, even the violence on the popular radio show *The Lone Ranger.*

The increase in juvenile delinquency during the War was dramatic. During the first full year, 1942, the rate of juvenile delinquency rose 8 per cent among boys and an astounding 31 per cent among girls. The increase of delinquency among girls was accounted for largely by sexual misbehavior, attributed to the "khakiwacky" teenagers who hung around drugstores, bus depots and other places where servicemen on leave usually congregated. These girls were known as "patriotutes" or "Victory girls" because, as one observer wrote, out of "a misguided sense of patriotism [she] believes she is contributing to the war effort by giving herself to the man in uniform."

Victory girls were not just promiscuous but aggressively so. In Detroit, the Navy had to build a fence around its armory to keep out V-girls. In San Antonio, a social worker reported that prostitutes were angry at "the young chippies" because they were "cramping their style." And in New York City, social workers reported that more than 60 per cent of the cases of venereal disease among soldiers had been contracted from girls under 21.

To many Americans, teen-age promiscuity seemed to signal a general decline in moral standards. They found confirmation of that belief in the public dalliances of actor Errol Flynn, who seemed to have a preference for very young women. In 1943, Flynn was charged with statutory rape by two 17-year-old girls. But his canny lawyer attacked the character of the plaintiffs, and Flynn was acquitted.

Public concern about delinquency among young people frequently focused less on their sexual morals than on their clothing. Some young men wore an outlandish costume known as the zoot suit, which had overstuffed shoulders and a jacket that reached almost down to the knees. The coat was worn unbuttoned to reveal baggy trousers that tapered from 16 inches wide at the knee to 6 inches at the

A Mexican-American youth in Los Angeles wears a popular nonmilitary garb of the early '40s—a zoot suit, complete with a thigh-length, broad-lapelled jacket and baggy trousers pegged at the cuff, topped off by a broad-brimmed felt hat. The City Council made the wearing of zoot suits a misdemeanor after servicemen and police clashed with zoot-suiters in June 1943 in a series of riots that had ugly racial overtones.

pegged bottom and a key chain that almost dragged on the floor. Zoot-suiters often carried switchblade knives and their girl friends packed whiskey flasks shaped to fit inside a bra. Under a wide-brimmed felt hat the zoot-suit wearer usually sported a hairstyle described by one reporter as "of increasing density and length at the neck."

The zoot suit, which originated among teenagers in Harlem and other urban slums, became a widespread fad. A song helped enhance its popularity: "I wanna zoot suit with a reat pleat/With a drape shape and a stuff cuff." To some observers, the zoot suit was a harmless emblem indicative of the desire to wear gaudy plumage before drab Army khaki replaced it. To others it was the uniform of young street gangs, an affront to the established order, a symbol of lawlessness—perhaps because of its association with minority youngsters, among whom the rate of juvenile delinquency was high.

Antagonism against the zoot suit reached its zenith in Los Angeles where the outfit was favored by the *pachucos*, teen-age Mexican-Americans who had acquired a reputation for toughness. A series of small-scale clashes in 1942 between zoot-suited pachucos and GIs provoked a crackdown by the county sheriff, who believed that Mexican-Americans had "a biological predisposition to criminal tendencies" because their ancestors, the Aztecs, had practiced human sacrifice. Then, in June 1943, a rumor spread that a sailor had been beaten up by a gang of pachucos. A mob of 2,500 soldiers and sailors gathered and, waging a "clean-up campaign," began pummeling some 100 young Mexican-Americans and ripping off their zoot suits. The Los Angeles City Council—in contrast to other communities where lawmakers dealt with teen-age violence by imposing a 10 p.m. curfew or by providing new recreational facilities—responded by outlawing the wearing of zoot suits.

In the long run no one on the home front was affected more deeply by the upheaval of World War II than America's 13 million blacks. For the blacks the War years marked a critical but agonizing period in the struggle for equality. Aroused at the outset by discriminatory hiring policies in defense industries and trade unions, and by the rigid segregation practiced in the armed services, blacks began to press effectively for their rights and in the process scored the first important civil rights victories since the period of post-Civil War Reconstruction.

In World War I, W. E. B. DuBois, cofounder of the National Negro Committee, which later became the National Association for the Advancement of Colored People (NAACP), had urged his fellow blacks to "forget our special grievances." Most had, at least, disregarded them. In World War II, however, blacks were determined to fight for democracy on two fronts—abroad and at home. Only this determination could overcome the cynicism and despair that many of them felt in the early days of the War. A student at a black college in the South spoke for many when he declared: "The Army jim crows us. The Navy lets us serve only as messmen. The Red Cross refuses our blood. Employers and labor unions shut us out. Lynchings continue. We are disenfranchised, jim crowed and spat upon. What more could Hitler do than that?"

As a matter of fact, a few blacks expressed an empathy not with the Germans but, because of their color, with the Japanese. "By the way, Captain," a sharecropper is said to have remarked to a plantation owner after Pearl Harbor, "I hear the Japs done declared war on you white folks." In New York City a poll of blacks revealed that 18 per cent believed they would be treated better under Japanese rule than in white America. Elijah Muhammad, the leader of the Black Muslims, was charged with sedition for his pro-Japanese sympathies and eventually served a four-year prison sentence for draft evasion.

Most black leaders, however, urged full participation in the war effort. They felt that if their people could work as equals, American society would reward them with equal rights. The first major move in this direction came in the months before Pearl Harbor when blacks were being excluded so blatantly from the defense labor build-up that one aircraft company had only 10 blacks among its 33,000 employees. In May 1941, A. Philip Randolph, president of the Brotherhood of Sleeping Car Porters, called on the federal government to ban discrimination in defense plants and threatened to lead a march on Washington on July 1. As the number of potential marchers escalated from 10,000 to 50,000, liberals and some black leaders tried to dissuade Randolph. Mrs. Eleanor Roosevelt, the blacks' most influential friend in Washington, told Randolph that such a march would be impractical because the hotels and restaurants in the nation's capital were not open to blacks.

But Randolph persisted. Five days before the scheduled march, President Roosevelt issued Executive Order 8802 that forbade racial discrimination in defense industries and established the Fair Employment Practices Commission to enforce the ban. Although the FEPC had the power only to investigate complaints, not to compel compliance, it immediately became a lightning rod for Southern hostility—one newspaper called it "dat cummittee fer de perteckshun of Rastus & Sambo." The FEPC proved able to resolve successfully only one third of the 8,000 complaints received, and

even legal compliance often took a bizarre turn toward total segregation. The Kingsbury Ordnance Plant in Indiana, which was constructed entirely with federal money, had a special production line for blacks, separate toilets and—the most preposterous indignity—a bomb shelter marked "for colored only." Nonetheless Roosevelt's Executive Order was a landmark—the first federal intercession on behalf of equal rights for blacks in three quarters of a century.

The planned march on Washington signaled a new turn in the civil rights struggle. For the first time a major protest had been planned to exclude white participation. In relying solely on the resources of the black community, the movement rekindled some of the mass enthusiasm sparked by the Jamaican-born black separatist Marcus Garvey in the 1920s. No longer, commented the conservative *Pittsburgh Courier,* would blacks make "the mistake of relying entirely upon the gratitude and sense of fair play of the American people."

The new black militancy fed on the hypocrisy of a nation that was waging war on totalitarianism abroad while maintaining segregation at home. The hypocrisy never seemed more ironic than in the case of privileges extended to some German prisoners of war who were interned in the U.S. In Salina, Kansas, for example, a black soldier went to a restaurant on the main street just to watch German POWs having lunch—and was reprimanded by the counterman. "You know we don't serve colored here," he was told. Of this incident, the soldier later wrote: "If we were *untermenschen* in Nazi Germany they would break our bones. As 'colored' men in Salina, they only break our hearts." When the black singer Lena Horne was invited to sing at a German POW camp she discovered that the camp commander had filled the front rows with prisoners and put the black guards in the blacks' traditional place—the back seats. She stepped down from the stage, strode up the aisle and, with her back turned defiantly to the Germans, sang for her own people.

The civil rights struggle at home was intensified by the bitter fact that black servicemen overseas often found that they were treated better by the local populace than by the whites at home or by their fellow GIs. In Britain, where fraternizing between blacks and local women sparked violent clashes among black and white American servicemen, British bystanders sometimes joined in on the side of the

Detroit policemen tangle with a rioter on February 28, 1942, a day of racial violence that exploded when white defense workers cordoned off a new federal housing project intended for black occupants. The riot was a prelude to a wave of race conflicts in 1943 in several American cities, including Detroit, where blacks endured poor housing and low income.

After a 25-mile hike in sweltering desert heat, soldiers of the 93rd Infantry Division, America's first all-black combat division, march in parade formation at Fort Huachuca, Arizona, in the summer of 1943. During the Second World War the majority of blacks in the Army served in segregated supply and construction units, which were not sent into combat.

blacks. A few pubs even practiced a kind of reverse discrimination, posting signs that read, "This House Is for Englishmen and Coloured American Troops Only."

Aroused by discrimination both in and out of the armed services, the heightened black consciousness pushed older organizations such as the NAACP to a new militancy and rapid gains in membership—during the War, NAACP membership increased ninefold, much of it in the South. The new black awareness also led to the formation of new groups such as the Congress of Racial Equality (CORE), which adapted the principles and tactics of nonviolent resistance that Gandhi practiced in India.

Among CORE's early leaders were James Farmer and Bayard Rustin, two young black pacifists who would figure

At the end of a harvest day in August 1944, three German prisoners of war begin the drive from the farm where they work to their nearby detainment camp in Hoopeston, Illinois. During World War II, more than 425,000 Axis POWs were held in the U.S. At the War's end, some fought deportation to homelands ravaged by war and stayed in America.

prominently in future integration battles. Their principal new weapon for desegregating restaurants and theaters in the North was the mass sit-in. In 1942, when a restaurant in downtown Chicago balked at serving blacks anything except sandwiches made of eggshells and garbage, CORE sent in a large biracial group to attempt to get seats. At first the restaurant refused to seat them, but finally an elderly white woman invited one of the blacks to share her table—to the applause of some 200 white diners who had tensely watched the drama.

The War years saw other gains, many in the entertainment field. All-black films began to appear regularly, and the hit of the 1943 Broadway season was *Othello,* starring Paul Robeson *(page 175).* On a more basic level, the Supreme Court, in 1944, outlawed all-white primary elections, thus taking the first step toward guaranteeing Southern blacks the right to vote.

Ironically, the economic gains that were scored during the War frequently served to fuel black impatience and discontent. While black employment rose by one million and the number of skilled workers doubled, the average black family's income by the end of the War still was only half that of the average white's. Moreover, living conditions remained substandard for most blacks. The paradox of progress feeding discontent, which social scientists would later label "the revolution of rising expectations," helped to set the scene for the rioting that rocked several American cities in 1943.

The worst outbreak—in fact, the worst race riot in the United States in 25 years—came in Detroit. Though things had been getting better for Detroit's blacks, especially for the 60,000 who had newly migrated from the South to find jobs in the war plants, most of them were boxed into the squalor of the ill-named Paradise Valley, a 60-block slum where sewage ran in the streets.

The frustrations of Detroit's blacks were concomitant with the growing resentment of working-class whites. Many of the whites were also newcomers from the South who had brought their prejudices with them. White workers regarded the growing prosperity of blacks as a threat to their own status—a fear skillfully played upon by the tracts of such hatemongers as Gerald L. K. Smith. Overcrowding—in housing, transportation and recreational facilities—multiplied the potential sources of friction.

On a steaming Sunday afternoon in June, racial fistfights broke out in a crowded municipal park on Belle Isle in the Detroit River. Rumors spread—a black man had supposedly raped and killed a white woman; whites had allegedly killed a black woman and her baby. Then came full-scale war. Blacks from nearby Paradise Valley smashed and looted white-owned stores. White mobs counterattacked. Before federal troops had forced a troubled peace on the area 36 hours later, nine whites and 25 blacks were dead. Seventeen of the blacks had been killed by the police.

The bloodshed in Detroit and other riot-afflicted cities—Springfield, Massachusetts; El Paso and Port Arthur, Texas; Hubbard, Ohio; Harlem—had at least one salutary effect. It stirred nationwide concern about the race problem. More than 200 cities and towns set up interracial committees. And the public opinion polls indicated that whites were beginning to wake up to the old discontent and the new militancy of black Americans. In 1942, a year before the riots, 62 per cent of the whites interviewed believed that blacks were "pretty well satisfied with things in this country." In 1944, only 25 per cent felt that way.

Even in the armed services, which had black soldiers fighting abroad, progress was agonizingly slow. The seeds of change were sown, but meaningful results were a long time in coming.

In 1944, the Army ordered the desegregation of its training camp facilities, but the pace of compliance, especially in the South, was slow. Overseas, late that same year, when the Battle of the Bulge produced a shortage of infantry replacements, the Army took its first tentative step toward battlefield integration: it attached black platoons to white companies. But integration did not go beyond that. Black and white soldiers still were not mixed in combat or training outfits. It was not until after the War—July 26, 1948—that President Truman signed the order officially desegregating the armed forces.

MAKING DO WITH LITTLE

With many of its trucks pressed into service as ambulances, the Boston Record American uses horse-drawn wagons to make daily deliveries of the newspaper.

SCARCITY IN THE LAND OF PLENTY

To be living on the home front during the War was to experience almost daily the frustration of not being able to buy what you wanted, when you wanted it. Even with the coupons for rationed foods and goods, the money for a major purchase or the patience to wait in long lines, there was never quite enough to go around.

Auto makers were ordered to stop building family cars in 1942; gas was rationed, and tires—even retreads—were in short supply. Gone from store windows were new toasters and refrigerators, irons and washing machines—in fact, most household appliances. Meat eaters got by on an initial weekly ration of 28 ounces. Butter lovers were held to an average of 12 pounds a year, 25 per cent less than normal. Coffee drinkers made do on a pound every five weeks, less than a cup a day. The sugar ration averaged eight to 12 ounces a week. Cigarettes were hard to come by, because 30 per cent of production went to the military.

There was hoarding of scarce commodities—one man in New Jersey stashed away enough sugar to satisfy his sweet tooth for 577 years. Many storekeepers learned soon enough to "set aside" for favored customers, and for a price, goods not readily available.

Most Americans, however, fortified their patience, drew on the old Yankee ingenuity and made do. They patched up aging cars, drove slower and shared rides. Their motoring reined in, they jammed railroads, which in 1942 turned a profit on passenger traffic for the first time in 15 years. Housewives used saccharin and corn syrup instead of sugar and stretched meats with all sorts of casseroles. Smokers revived the "roll-your-own" cigarette, and coffee drinkers rebrewed grounds. Neighbors shared appliances.

The annoyance of shortages was compounded by the amount of money ready to be spent—more than $90 billion more in the pockets of consumers in 1944 than at the time of Pearl Harbor. In general, though, spirits remained high. Home-front sacrifices stirred a sense of duty. Victory was coming. The promise of plenty made scantily stocked grocery shelves, and even empty auto showrooms, tolerable.

To save gas and rubber, a 35-mph speed limit was imposed; commuters formed car pools, and driving alone produced a touch of guilt.

Although the basic gasoline ration for pleasure driving permitted only three to five gallons a week, drivers often discovered that the pumps had run dry.

THE STRUGGLE TO REMAIN MOBILE

When the War Production Board banned the manufacture of private automobiles in February 1942, the order had the impact of a bomb on American motorists. There were more than 27 million cars on the road and an inventory of barely half a million replacements. In addition, with industry geared up to make vehicles for military use, spare parts for the civilian market became virtually unobtainable.

The result was a frantic campaign by car owners and the government, in the slogan of the times, to "Keep 'em Rolling." Drivers wore tire treads down to the cord and scavenged junk yards for everything from intake valves to exhaust pipes. Tire and gas rationing, introduced in 1942, saved equipment by reducing automobile mileage one third by 1943.

America's inventors got into the act, too. There were engine modifications to save gas, and wooden wheels—usually on delivery trucks—to save rubber. One tinkerer produced a wheel that was made of steel springs covered with layers of paper. And in Newport, Rhode Island, a dowager got around town in a beach chair propelled by a motorcycle.

As a result of its conservation measures, America did keep rolling: the number of passenger cars in use at the peak of the war effort was off only 12.9 per cent from what it was in 1941.

A driver sets a torch to the charcoal-burning generator that helped to power his truck with methane.

Two pairs of hardwood tires—one set new, the other driven 500 miles—are displayed by a mechanic.

A straining wife pushes as her husband steers the family car out of the garage. The car's reverse gear was broken, and replacement parts were unavailable.

Soldiers on weekend furlough line up with civilians for bus tickets at a station in Columbus, Georgia. Military personnel had first call on transportation.

THE CRUSH OF WARTIME TRAVEL

If the car was broken, the tires bald or the gasoline ration expended, there was always public transportation. But millions of travelers had the same idea.

Virtually every train station, bus depot and airport in the country was jammed with military personnel on the move between training camps, military posts and ports of embarkation. The railroads carried 97 per cent of the traffic, transporting two million men a month, more than 43 million *in toto*. Troop movements required half of all Pullman space, relegating weary civilians to fretful nights in cramped coach seats. Troop trains, some with white flags denoting them "specials," churned from coast to coast and forced parlor-car riders onto sidings for hours on end. A scheduled overnight's journey from New York to Chi-cago invariably got the weary traveler to his destination by lunch instead of break-fast—and often as late as dinner.

The government begged foot-loose civilians to stay at home. "The time is here," warned the Office of Defense Transportation in 1942, "when all must realize that unnecessary travel can seriously harm the war effort." But travel volume, necessary or not, was huge. In 1944, railroads logged three times as many passenger miles as in 1941; intercity buses, more than twice as many miles as in prewar days.

Riders endured cattle-car conditions—and were grateful even for standing room. There was a brisk trade in black-market Pullman reservations. Scalpers sold tickets at markups of $10 to $50; tourist agencies added $20 "service charges" to reservations. All told, the War meant unprecedented travel turmoil. An ad for the Atlantic Coast Line Railroad said, correctly: "You'll be more comfortable at home."

Packed shoulder to shoulder, riders on a Southern Railway coach log some of the 55 billion passenger miles tallied on trains in the United States in 1942.

A crowd of shivering Bostonians surrounds a dealer as he doles out precious heating oil in 1942. The policeman was on hand to help regulate distribution.

PLEASURES NO LONGER TAKEN FOR GRANTED

Americans choosing to stay at home often found life uncomfortable there, too. During the icy winter of 1942-1943, fuel rationing was begun, and consumers were allotted about two thirds of their 1941 consumption—barely enough to heat homes to 65°. The situation became so severe in the Northeast that Connecticut launched a campaign to list all wood lots where residents could cut kindling and logs to burn in stoves and fireplaces.

Everyday items of convenience or self-indulgence, long taken for granted, were hard to come by—liquor, laundry soap, facial tissue, cotton diapers, thumbtacks and hair curlers. Nylon had "gone to war," and women went back to stockings of rayon and cotton. In late 1944, most stores had to post "No Cigarettes" signs. But many did have black-market "stoopies"—"the kind you stoop down behind the counter for."

The shortage that hurt people most involved a staple—meat. In New York, beef stocks were 35 per cent of normal. Boston, used to a million pounds a day, received three carloads instead of its normal 75. Housewives in almost every U.S. city found themselves with meat ration coupons to spare, but nothing to buy.

The alternatives were to patronize the black-market butchers, who got an estimated 20 per cent of the beef, or to locate substitutes. Unrationed and going for 20 cents a pound, horsemeat became a replacement for beef, which cost 55 cents a pound or more. Some restaurants began to serve buffalo, antelope and even beaver meat. *Gourmet* magazine soon joined the trend: "Although it isn't/Our usual habit,/ This year we're eating/The Easter Rabbit."

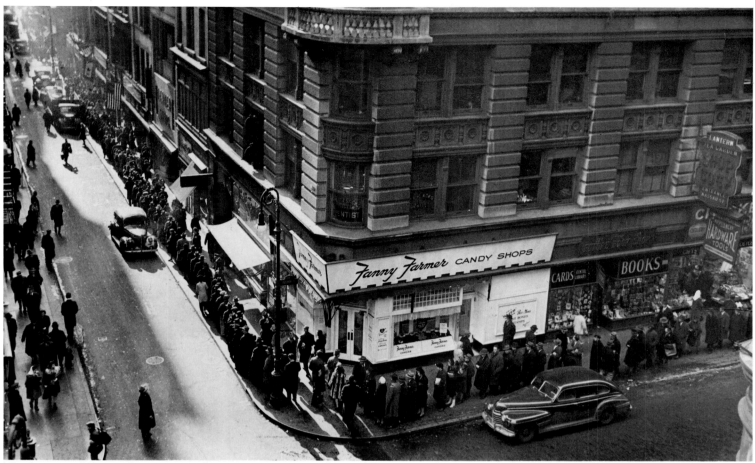

Nicotine-starved New Yorkers queue up for scarce cigarettes at Fulton and Nassau streets in 1944. Each customer was allowed to purchase only two packs.

Pleased with her find, a woman slips right into a pair of nylon hose.

The Man-O-War Packing Co. in Newark, New Jersey, features horsemeat.

A Washington, D.C., couple solves the housing shortage with a houseboat.

Used houses, ready for purchase, are inspected by a family in Los Angeles.

A CRUNCH ON LIVING SPACE

The most stubborn and ubiquitous shortage of all was housing, with 98 per cent of U.S. cities reporting insufficient single-family houses and 90 per cent unable to meet apartment needs. Workers streaming to booming defense towns were greeted with "No Vacancy" signs. The lucky shared rooms with other new arrivals or moved into rows of jerry-built boxes of plywood and plasterboard. The unlucky resorted to tents and even shelters nailed together out of packing cases.

For some, such makeshift dwellings became "home." When social workers asked a man to move his large family from a tent to a government-housing unit, he refused: "What's good enough for the boys in Africa," he said, "is good enough for me."

Hungry workers from an aircraft plant dig into a meal served at an overcrowded

boardinghouse in San Diego. Public War Housing Centers scrounged communities for unused space and urged householders to double up and rent spare rooms.

WONDERFUL TOWN

Sailors on shore leave from the battleship U.S.S. North Carolina, accompanied by a civilian, possibly a journalist, cross New York Harbor to Manhattan on a launch

THE GLITTERING ALLURE OF OLD BROADWAY

The pressures and tensions of the War created a need for escape among hard-working people on the home front—and one of the best places to get away from it all was New York City. There was more opportunity for enjoyment per square inch along the streets of midtown Manhattan than anywhere else in the country, and servicemen in particular took full advantage of it. They swarmed over Times Square and Broadway, New York's "Great White Way," in search of live entertainment and the company of pretty girls. New York, in turn, came alive in a way never seen before.

About 200 restaurants, serving some five million meals a week, catered to Times Square's bustling tourist trade. An evening was hardly complete without a slice of Lindy's famous cheesecake or a cheese blintz at one of Broadway's many delicatessens. Over 50 nightclubs such as El Morocco and the Stork Club provided drinks and dancing to the music of the big bands, and audiences thrilled to the voice of a young crooner by the name of Frank Sinatra, who was appearing at the Paramount Theater. The Copacabana headlined Jimmy Durante, the proud possessor of the greatest proboscis on Broadway.

Scores of movie houses showed first-run films dramatizing morale-boosting war themes. Often, as in the comedy *See Here, Private Hargrove (sign, right)*, the movies were simply adaptations of best sellers or of plays that had already proved their appeal on the New York stage. With many Broadway attractions offering free tickets or discount rates for servicemen, the size of audiences swelled. In 1943 alone more than 11 million people attended Broadway shows. The demand was so great that the drama critic for *The New York Times* commented with acerbity: "It was a public so anxious to attend the theater that for a time it would attend anything playing in a theater. Some of the managers took advantage of this and offered plays which, in normal years, would never have passed Bridgeport." Not that it mattered, for the excitement alone of an evening on Broadway was more than enough to make a serviceman's excursion to New York City worthwhile.

Theater, government and military officials in 1942 check a list of Broadway theater attractions for which tickets were available to officers at half-price.

Colorful billboards and marquees dominate the Great White Way at Times Square, New York City's popular center for movies, plays, dining and danc

GOING ALL OUT FOR THE BOYS IN UNIFORM

Broadway greeted its wartime guests graciously, offering the boys in uniform everything from benefit shows to chances to appear in shows themselves. The cast of Rodgers and Hammerstein's musical *Oklahoma!* put on 44 free performances for servicemen only, while Irving Berlin's *This Is the Army* boasted a "Cast of 300 Soldiers" in a rousing spectacle of Army life set to music.

One of Broadway's most successful wartime efforts was the Stage Door Canteen, which opened in the basement of the 44th Street Theater in 1942 to a long line of enlisted men thrilled to find a place in the big city where they could live it up with the stars. As many as 2,200 hostesses were on call to keep the men company and offer such all-American treats as doughnuts and milk, while celebrities on the order of Gypsy Rose Lee, Ethel Merman, Marlene Dietrich, Alfred Lunt and Lynn Fontanne entertained them. Seven other Stage Door Canteens opened across the U.S., but the original remained the most famous one. A weekly radio program was broadcast from it, and a movie—inevitably a love story—was made about it.

Servicemen join actress Tallulah Bankhead in song at New York's Stage Door Canteen.

The program book of the movie Stage Door Canteen features hostesses and soldiers.

UNCLE SAM
presents

IRVING BERLIN'S
ALL SOLDIER SHOW
"THIS IS THE ARMY"

CAST OF 300 SOLDIERS
PROCEEDS TO ARMY EMERGENCY RELIEF FUND

A poster for Irving Berlin's This Is the Army touts its stars: soldiers from all over the U.S.

Veteran Berlin, in his 1918 uniform, rehearses with the GI cast.

A soldier shows his form as a dancing waitress.

TREADING THE BOARDS IN THE THEATER OF WAR

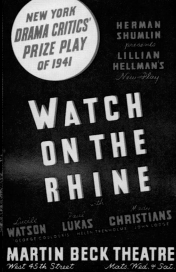

In Lillian Hellman's play Watch on the Rhine, an American and her German husband take refuge with her mother.

A soldier falls in love in Broadway's long-running comedy The Voice of the Turtle.

In the 1945 comedy Dear Ruth, a GI comes home to find he has been writing not to Ruth, but to her younger sister.

An all-black cast brings Anna Lucasta, a drama about a prostitute's liaisons with sailors, to Broadway in 1944.

The Broadway theaters did more than welcome servicemen to their performances; they took the War as the subject of many of their finest productions. Works by such authors as John Hersey and Lillian Hellman were based on war themes or actual incidents out of the War. The plays reflected the audiences' concern not just with the world conflict, but with the careers and romances of individual soldiers. Whether cast as a lover or a leader, a man in uniform possessed an immediate heroic appeal that civilians, as well as servicemen, could understand and applaud.

FREDRIC MARCH

as Major Joppolo
in

A Bell for Adano

CORT THEATRE

Fredric March (poster and seated, above left) projects military authority as Major Joppolo, an American serving as military administrator of an Italian town, in the 1944 play A Bell for Adano.

Alexandra Danilova of the Ballet Russe de Monte Carlo, which attracted many GIs, dances Swan Lake in a triple exposure taken in 1942.

Judith Anderson and Maurice Evans enact the coronation scene of Macbeth. The ruthless king's treachery seemed particularly apt in 1942.

ENTERTAINMENT IN THE CLASSIC MODE

The New York theaters' offerings during the War years included not only contemporary drama and music, but also classic works—everything from opera and ballet to Shakespearean tragedies. World-famous ballet dancers, including the corps of the Ballet Russe de Monte Carlo, who had fled Europe, were now performing before audiences in New York City.

In keeping with the times, the works presented had war themes or appropriate messages. Program notes sometimes called attention to parallels with ongoing world events and conditions—or such villains as Adolf Hitler.

PAUL ROBESON

as

OTHELLO

THE MOOR OF VENICE

As this production of "Othello" begins, we are in the middle of a year and in the middle of a war; and when at war, it may not be out of place to keep other wars, of other times in mind. For, by this means, patterns and directions may be the clearer. We are now engaged in a war to protect a way of life which we feel offers the greatest benefit to the greatest number of people. Venice in the Sixteenth Century was fighting too; her wars were to protect Christianity in the Eastern Mediterranean.

In our conflict, all races are allied to fight for common ideals. The Negro pilot of the Army Air Corps may fly under the command of Chiang in China; just as soldiers of other races fought with Venice for the protection of Christianity.

The program for the 1943 revival of Othello includes a note explaining the significance of the play for a wartime audience, especially in terms of its racial implications. As Othello, Paul Robeson (right) received one of the longest ovations in New York theater history.

Michael Todd presents
ETHEL MERMAN
in
SOMETHING
FOR THE BOYS
Staged by
HASSARD SHORT
Book by HERBERT and DOROTHY FIELDS
—with—
ALLEN JENKINS
COLE PORTER SONGS
Souvenir Book

Ethel Merman (center stage), in the 1943 musical
Something for the Boys, plays the unlikely
role of an ex-chorus girl whose carborundum
dental work turns her into a human radio.
Cole Porter's score bolstered the thin plot.

STAR-SPANGLED SPECTACLES TO LIGHT UP THE STAGE

Musicals with large casts had always been
a hallmark of the Broadway theater, but
now with greater box-office receipts and
a demand for escapist entertainment, they
became bigger and splashier. Their eye-
catching spectacles and bouncy tunes elic-
ited patriotic feelings and helped keep up
morale on the home front. The 1943 musical Something for the Boys boasted, in ad-

dition to a wealth of Cole Porter tunes
belted out by Ethel Merman, a glee club of
servicemen, an on-stage Army Air Forces
band and a fast-stepping female chorus.
Even some of the more serious plays like
Winged Victory went in for star-spangled
moments when the entire cast assembled
on stage and audiences were stirred to
bursts of appreciative applause.

Three sailors in On the Town ride the subway in search of "Miss Turnstiles," only to discover she is a hootchy-kootchy dancer (above left)

Sophie Tucker, "The Last of the Red-Hot Mammas," assumes a patriotic Statue of Liberty pose and leads a burlesque troupe in High Kickers

a dramatic moment from Broadway's 1943 hit Winged Victory

training. The play, which took its title from the Greek statue The Winged Victory of Samothrace depicted on the program (inset), garnered raves from critics.

6

World War II was a period of explosive growth for the United States. The population reached 140 million during the War, up nearly eight million from 1940. The federal budget soared to a staggering $98.4 billion, more than 10 times the nine-billion-dollar budget of 1939. The gross national product—the measure of the nation's total production of goods and services—made an unprecedented leap to $213 billion, up from $90 billion in 1939. The total labor force grew to an all-time high of 66 million. U.S. farms harvested a phenomenal 5.5 billion bushels of corn, oats and wheat. College and university enrollment was climbing toward 1.7 million from a prewar high of 1.4 million.

In nearly all its cultural and economic institutions, the U.S. took a quantum leap out of the past. Science, once the realm of men and women puttering in lonely laboratories, became inextricably linked with the nation's technology, supported by government dollars and pursued by task forces of the country's best brains. Federal outlays for scientific research and development increased from $74 million in 1940 to an all-time high of $1.6 billion in 1945.

Foremost among the burgeoning institutions was the government itself. The number of federal employees swelled from one million to 3.8 million—increasing 300 per cent since 1939—and together they earned a giant paycheck of more than seven billion dollars a year. The bulk of these employees worked in Washington—the population of the District of Columbia mushroomed from a little more than 900,000 in 1940 to 1.3 million in 1944. But federal employees were also strung out all across the land. Nearly a quarter of a million worked in New York City and its environs; 170,000 were employed in Philadelphia. Paper work both inside and outside the government proliferated accordingly. "We are expected to fill out 17 forms, reports and questionnaires a month to government agencies," grumbled a Knoxville foundry operator in a letter addressed to "Your Excellency" at the White House. "So around and around we go," he continued. "Is there any hope for relief?"

There was not much. By 1945 the government had insinuated itself into virtually every phase of the nation's life. It now functioned more or less in partnership with industry, labor, farming, medicine, education and science.

After the government, the biggest growth occurred in the field of business and industry. As production rose to meet

DAYS OF DAZZLING GROWTH

the War's needs, so did corporate earnings—and with them the means for still further expansion. Corporate profits in 1943 totaled $8.5 billion, a jump of $2.1 million over the prewar level. Most of the companies that shared in the business boom were directly involved in war production; Curtiss-Wright, for instance, was able to grow from a small company in 1939 to the nation's second largest aircraft manufacturer because it helped fill the government's demand for airplanes. But any company that could find a way to relate its product to the War also stood to profit. The Parker Company, as producers of pens and ink, had nothing strategic to offer the government. Nevertheless, by advertising that everyone on the home front could help the war effort by writing lonely servicemen at camp and abroad, Parker touched a responsive chord in the public—and boosted sales of its ink by 800 per cent.

Ironically, for an administration that had attempted to control business, the government now allowed the antitrust laws to languish for the duration of the crisis. On the eve of the War, so important a corporation as the Standard Oil Company of New Jersey—in violation not only of the Sherman Antitrust Act, but also of the national interest—made a private deal with I. G. Farbenindustrie, the large German chemical firm, to forego the development of synthetic rubber, in exchange for a promise from Farben to keep its petroleum products out of the U.S. market. It was largely because of this unorthodox pact that the U.S. lagged perilously behind Germany in the development of synthetic rubber in 1941—the very time when Japanese conquests in Southeast Asia were making it impossible for the U.S. to get natural rubber from the Dutch Indies. Yet when the deal was exposed, Thurman Arnold, who as Assistant Attorney General four years earlier had been given a franchise by Roosevelt to enforce the antitrust laws, had his hand stayed. Standard Oil was required to pay a minimal fine—and then was promptly forgiven by the government and the public.

Arnold later recalled the episode with a certain cynicism. "The representatives of big business filtered into the War and Navy Departments and the War Production Board," he wrote. "And F.D.R., recognizing that he could have only one war at a time, was content to declare a truce in the fight against monopoly. He was to have his foreign war; monopoly was to give him patriotic support—on its own terms."

Another official at the Justice Department took it more philosophically. "The big guys could deliver, and got bigger," he said.

As business waxed ever bigger and stronger, so did its traditional adversary, labor. Like business, it did so with a helping hand from the government. In the 1930s, the New Deal had given labor a giant boost with the Wagner Act, which guaranteed workers the right to organize without management interference and to bargain collectively. Now, with the War, labor was favored by further government action through a ruling that legalized a so-called "maintenance of membership" plan. Under it, a new worker at an already-unionized plant had to join the union unless he formally resigned within 15 days of being employed. The ruling was a compromise that fell short of labor's demands for a closed shop—but it proved to be an impressive stimulus to the unions' growth. While the total labor force increased by 22 per cent during the War years, union membership grew by 45 per cent—going from 10.5 million in 1939 to 14.75 million in 1945. A measure of labor's growing power was evident in 1944, when the unions delivered a bloc vote to the Democrats for the first time in history. During the campaign, labor also made a munificent contribution of two million dollars, which constituted 30 per cent of the Democratic campaign treasury.

Nobody on the home front benefited more from the nation's wartime growth than the farmer. Total farm income in 1945 reached an unprecedented $24 billion—an increase of 250 per cent over 1939—as production went way up. And surprisingly, this burst of prosperity occurred in spite of a tremendous loss of some 800,000 workers.

There were many reasons why agriculture prospered as it did. One was the Lend-Lease Act, which sent quantities of foodstuffs overseas. Another was parity, the government subsidy designed to bring agricultural prices into balance with industrial prices. Based on a formula that related to crop prices before World War I, when the farmers enjoyed a heyday, parity guaranteed farmers that their purchasing power would never fall below a certain percentage of that of industrial workers. Parity steadily mounted during the War, reaching a peak of 110 per cent in 1943. Initially, it covered only six basic crops, such as wheat, corn and cotton, the production of which the government sought to encourage; but by 1943 a farmer could grow virtually any crop he wished and still be protected by subsidy.

There were other important reasons for the growth in agricultural income. Farmers were now farming more economically and getting larger yields from their crops. Advances in scientific knowledge had brought them better fertilizers and feeds. In the 1940s the average consumption of commercial fertilizer came to more than double that of the 1930s, having risen from 6.6 million tons to 13.6 million tons; simultaneously, the corn yield went from 40 bushels an acre to 50 bushels. Similarly, with nutritionally improved feed formulas containing a greater volume of protein, dairy cows gave more milk, hens laid more eggs, and hogs, sheep and steers put on more meat for every pound of feed that they ate.

An even greater boost to farm production resulted from mechanization. Between 1940 and 1945 the number of tractors on American farms rose from 1.5 million to 2.4 million, a jump of 53 per cent. Together with a corresponding rise in the number of trucks, grain combines, cotton pickers, milking machines, hay dehydrators and flame cultivators, the new machines resulted in an average saving of 240 million man-hours a year between 1939 and 1944—and an increase of 29 per cent in gross production per worker. In 1945 the average farmer produced enough to feed himself and 13 other people, as opposed to nine in 1940.

Meanwhile, the American farm itself was growing slowly but significantly bigger. All together, farm sizes increased an average of 10 per cent during the War. But the growth was uneven; in farming as in industry, the big got bigger while the small lost out. Between 1940 and 1945 the acreage under cultivation in holdings of 50 to 100 acres or more grew by 94 million acres. Before long, farming would come to be known as agribusiness—commercial farming done on a large scale, often by corporations instead of lone individuals—and farmers would have to be knowledgeable in an increasing variety of complex subjects, which included economics, engineering and science.

One of the most surprising spurts of growth during the War occurred in the nation's educational institutions. At the outset, it had appeared that colleges and universities, like the farms, stood to lose their young men to the draft. The number of law school graduates in June 1944 came to only one fifth that of prewar days, while the number of liberal arts graduates was down by about half. Some institutions expected to have to close.

But the Cassandras predicting doom were in for a surprise. For the armed forces suddenly faced the problem of training thousands of new recruits in such recondite subjects as ballistics, cartography, metallurgy, cryptanalysis and aeronautics. To do so they turned to the colleges and universities. By the end of 1943 the Army Specialized Training Program (ASTP) had 140,000 soldiers enrolled on college campuses; the Navy College Training Program, or V-12, had 80,000. By the War's end 1.5 million men had been to college at federal expense.

Through the ASTP and V-12, colleges and universities made up what they had lost in private tuitions. These programs, however, were destined to last only until the end of the War. What then? Fortunately, the federal government, in its urgency to stay a jump ahead of the enemy in armaments, looked to universities for advanced research, just as it looked to industry for the manufacture of the tools of war—and in supporting this research, it enabled the universities to expand and improve facilities.

The lion's share of the government's contracts went to the Massachusetts Institute of Technology, which earned a

The first successful U.S. Army helicopter, the YR-4A, flies past the Capitol dome on May 30, 1943, to celebrate the 25th anniversary of regular U.S. airmail service—and inaugurate a new era in aviation. Designed by Igor Sikorsky, the helicopter was known in the Army Air Forces as the "Flying Windmill." Destined to play a major role as a troop carrier in America's future wars, it was still too tricky to maneuver easily and too small to be of much military use in World War II. Looking ahead to peace, developers billed it as a substitute for the family car.

spectacular $117 million for doing a major part of the research that led to 150 different radar systems. Close behind in funding came the California Institute of Technology, Columbia, Harvard and Princeton, which developed rockets, explosives, napalm and ballistics. The contracts provided not only for salaries and materials, but also for the construction of new laboratories and the expansion of old ones; and the updated labs with all their equipment were to revert to the schools when the War ended. Once again, the big got bigger.

Meanwhile, the War was imposing such heavy demands on the nation's scientific community that, in 1941, Roosevelt created the Office of Scientific Research and Development to coordinate the competing demands. Vannevar Bush, a mathematician and a former vice president of M.I.T., was put in charge. As head of the OSRD, Bush commanded the services of some 30,000 physicists, chemists, doctors, lawyers, business managers, generals, admirals, laborers and civil servants—as motley a combination as ever was crowded under a single umbrella. Together they scored some incredible achievements.

Though much wartime scientific research was perforce directed toward the wholesale destruction of the enemy, a good deal also went toward the preservation of human life. U.S. government funds financed and brought into widespread use two lifesaving discoveries that had lain dormant for many years. One was the insecticide dichlorodiphenyltrichloroethane, a synthetic compound formulated in 1874 by a German chemistry student and then never put to use. American researchers in the Surgeon General's office and OSRD revived the compound and called it DDT. Sprayed in massive quantities, it eliminated the lice and mosquitoes that were causing epidemics of typhus and malaria among the troops in the Mediterranean and the Pacific.

The other long-neglected discovery—and the one that was to prove the single most spectacular medical advance of the War—was penicillin. In 1928 a British researcher, Dr. Alexander Fleming, had found that *Penicillium,* a type of mold much like that found on household bread and cheese, would destroy bacteria. From the mold Dr. Fleming extracted the essential substance and named it penicillin. Further developed and improved by the U.S. Department of Agriculture laboratory at Peoria, Illinois, penicillin was then mass-produced by American industry. The new antibiotic was used during the War to treat blood poisoning and infections from battle wounds. It joined a pharmacopoeia that now included improved sulfa drugs, which a serviceman could carry in his first-aid pouch and administer to himself, and dried blood plasma, which when mixed with distilled water could be transfused by medics on the battlefield. Together these medical advances helped to keep alive 97 per cent of the U.S. servicemen wounded in battle.

Of all the scientific achievements of the War, the biggest and most significant by far was, of course, the making of the atom bomb. Though its explosion took the world by surprise in 1945, its creation was the work of hundreds of thousands of hands, representing a monumental collaboration of military, industrial and scholarly interests.

For a decade or more, many of the world's best scientific minds had been addressing their attention to theoretical physics. In Rome in 1934, Enrico Fermi, experimenting with uranium, had demonstrated that the atom could be split by bombarding the nucleus with slow-moving neutrons. Lise Meitner, a Viennese physicist who had fled with her nephew and collaborator Otto Frisch to Copenhagen following the German take-over of Austria, determined that the combined weight of the two halves of the split uranium atom was less than the original mass; and that the missing mass had been transformed into energy.

Danish physicist Niels Bohr carried news of the Meitner-Frisch achievement to a physicists' meeting in Washington, D.C., on January 26, 1939. So electrifying was the effect on the world community of physicists that before the end of the year nearly 100 academic papers had been published on the subject.

Meanwhile, in the summer of 1939 a newspaper story with no particular significance for most readers caught the eye of physicists: Germany had forbidden the export of uranium from Czechoslovakia, a country that claimed one of the world's few known deposits of the element. To physicists, the embargo on uranium meant only one thing. Germany must be working on an atom bomb.

One of the first scientists to take alarm was Fermi, who after being awarded the Nobel Prize in 1938 had emigrated to the United States. He tried to alert the U.S. government to the danger of Germany's developing an atom bomb, but his warnings went unheeded. Beset by mounting apprehension, he and two other fugitive physicists—Leo Szilard and Eugene P. Wigner, both from Hungary—turned to Albert Einstein, whose eminence just might give him entree to top political circles. Although Einstein was later to regret his involvement with the bomb, in 1939 he agreed to Szilard's pleas to address a letter to President Roosevelt sketching the history of the experiments with uranium. The letter suggested that the Germans might already have gone beyond such experiments and be building a bomb big enough to blow up a "whole port, together with the surrounding territory." In order to make sure that the letter would reach the President himself and not be thrown away by some intermediary, the scientists entrusted its delivery to Alexander Sachs, a Wall Street financier and occasional adviser to Roosevelt.

When Sachs was received at the White House in October, six weeks after the German invasion of Poland, he took no chances on the President's missing the purpose of his visit. He read the letter aloud. Even then the letter almost failed to strike home; its discursive ramblings and abstract theories bored the President. But Sachs was determined not to give up. Pressing his point, he reminded Roosevelt that Napoleon had dismissed as impractical the invention of the steamship—thereby losing a potential means of invading England. With that inspired analogy, the President swiftly got the message and exclaimed, "What you are after is to see that the Nazis don't blow us up." He produced a bottle of spirits suitable to the occasion—Napoleon brandy—and filled a glass for himself and one for Sachs. Then he summoned his military aide, Brigadier General Edwin "Pa" Watson. Waving the letter at Watson, the President told him, "Pa, this requires action."

The action began modestly with the formation of the Advisory Committee on Uranium in the fall of 1939 and continued somewhat desultorily for two years. After the attack on Pearl Harbor, research picked up and, under the code name of Manhattan Project, an all-out effort was launched with the ultimate object of building a bomb. Eventually the undertaking was to disburse some two billion dollars through more than 1,200 contracts, assigned to more than 25 universities and upward of 37 industrial enterprises. The project involved 120,000 people in 19 states and Canada.

The Manhattan Project was headed by Brigadier General Leslie B. Groves, a regular Army officer with a tidy mind and what one contemporary described as "the most impressive ego since Napoleon." Groves had little time for humor. He had never worked with scientists before and told his military staff: "We have gathered here the largest collection of crackpots ever seen." But his stern no-nonsense approach was just what was called for in a two-billion-dollar enterprise that President Truman was later to describe as "the greatest scientific gamble in history."

The universities and industrial plants involved in the Manhattan Project faced a number of seemingly impossible tasks. One was the procurement of sufficient materials for their experiments. Uranium is among the scarcest of elements, and only one of its rarer forms, the isotope U-235, was thought to be unstable enough to split. Fortunately, in 1942 the U.S. had a stockpile of 1,200 tons of uranium oxide from the Belgian Congo, which it had seized when the Germans invaded Belgium, as well as another 500 tons of uranium wastes produced by metal refineries in the Rockies. Under the urging of Dr. Arthur Compton, who was head of the University of Chicago's research laboratory, the Lamp Division of the Westinghouse Electric Corporation started utilizing these supplies to step up its production of purified uranium.

The second major problem was that of establishing a fission reaction on a scale sufficient to produce an explosion. Fermi solved this problem by creating a self-sustaining chain reaction—wherein the splitting of each atom triggered the splitting of other atoms. A third and equally complex problem was that of taking the chain reaction and putting it to work in a bomb.

Any of these goals would have been elusive enough in the best of circumstances; as it was, the scientists were harried by a host of fears, worries and frustrations. One concern was the desperate need for speed; the revolutionary ground they were treading had to be covered at breakneck pace, for Germany, still leading the world in planes and submarines, was thought to have at least a year's jump on the developing atom bomb. Another concern was the need for secrecy. Many scientists endured censored mail

THE POSITIVE SIDE OF WAR: ACHIEVEMENTS FOR PEACE

With bulbs giving off as much heat as four card players, air conditioning's effect is shown by smoke-treated cool air rising from the floor.

This computer at M.I.T.—introduced in 1942 —weighed 100 tons, had 2,000 electronic tubes, 150 electric motors and 200 miles of wire.

Naval radar search patterns are plotted on a luminous screen. The revolving electronic eye could extend vision more than 200 miles.

A technician at Harvard Medical School scrapes powdered blood substances into a jar. Other plasma components stand on shelves.

Out of the Second World War were to come a host of advancements in science and technology that not only affected the outcome of the fighting, but also would change life in America when the fighting was over. Most of the refinements, coordinated and sponsored by the government's multibillion-dollar Office of Scientific Research and Development, were aimed at winning the War. Yet even military innovations—nuclear research, improvements in telecommunications, aerodynamics and radar—had peacetime implications. Radar, for example, growing from fledgling status to a three-billion-dollar industry by 1945, was to revolutionize commercial aviation.

War-spurred production breakthroughs were to make many prewar luxuries, including air conditioning—and the magical novelty, television—readily available once factories could resume civilian production. New plastics and synthetics would find innumerable uses in postwar homes. And computers, pioneered at M.I.T. by Dr. Vannevar Bush in the 1930s and improved during the War, would father more and more scientific achievements in the years ahead.

The pace of medical research also accelerated during the War. Antibiotics, primarily penicillin, cut down dramatically on deaths from infected battle wounds. There were remarkable advances in blood chemistry. Plasma—the straw-colored liquid left when the red cells are filtered out of blood —could be freeze dried, vacuum packed, and sent to hospitals and medics. And in 1945, Harvard researchers separated plasma into its five component proteins, each with unique life-sustaining properties.

and tapped telephones. They were referred to by code names and trailed by bodyguards. Some were even forbidden to open checking accounts in local banks or to take out life insurance policies, lest their identities be revealed. Workmen on the project were kept in the dark about what they were doing. A foreman at a West Coast plant bespoke their bafflement when he told his men they were making "the front part of horses, to be shipped to Washington for final assembly."

Not the least cause of anxiety was the extreme danger involved in the experimental phase of the work. At the University of Chicago, where the all-important chain reaction was proceeding under Fermi's direction, three young physicists served on a suicide brigade; they stood on scaffolding above the reacting nuclear pile with pails of cadmium solution—which would absorb the neutrons and stop the reaction—at the ready. Their task would be to douse the uranium by hand if the automatic controls failed at the crucial instant when fission occurred. Otherwise the laboratory, the university, perhaps even the city of Chicago and its environs might be blasted off the map.

It was at this laboratory—an improvised workshop set up in an abandoned squash court beneath the football stadium—that the first nuclear chain reaction occurred, on the freezing cold afternoon of December 2, 1942. Fermi had been conducting the day's work since 9:45 a.m. before a hushed gathering of colleagues and students, all tense in the expectation that this would be the telling experiment. With an expressionless face he gave laconic instructions to move one rod of the reactor here, another one there. Suddenly at 3:30 p.m. he smiled broadly, shut his slide rule and announced with understated satisfaction, "The reaction is self-sustaining." Eugene Wigner, who was present, came up with a bottle of Chianti, which was passed around with paper cups, then signed by everyone there. When the celebration was over Dr. Compton called Harvard President James Conant. "Jim," he told his colleague in a code that his listener readily understood, "the Italian navigator has just landed in the New World."

The great scientific threshold had been crossed; now the burden switched from proving an academic hypothesis to engineering a bomb. That was no mean task in itself. Henry D. Smyth, a Princeton physicist who was one of the legion of scientists engaged in the work, asserted: "The technological gap between producing a controlled chain reaction and using it as a large-scale power source or an explosive is comparable to the gap between the discovery of fire and the manufacture of a steam locomotive." In human history that gap had extended about 700,000 years.

The building of the bomb necessitated the diversion of crucial scientific manpower from other vital war-related efforts, such as the production of synthetic rubber and high-octane gasoline, shipbuilding and the manufacture of other new weapons. It meant winning the cooperation of industry, without the promise of profits or the hope that patents would be given for new inventions devised in the process.

The work got under way at once all across the country. At a 59,000-acre tract on the Clinch and Tennessee rivers about 18 miles from Knoxville, two enormous plants went up for the separation of the U-235 isotope from uranium. The construction and outfitting of one suggested the heterogeneous nature of the industrial collaboration that was involved. The Stone and Webster Engineering Corporation constructed and assembled the plant; Westinghouse took on the manufacture of mechanical parts; General Electric supplied the electrical equipment; Allis-Chalmers turned out magnets; and Skidmore-Owings Merrill laid out the town for the workers, which was to be known as Oak Ridge and which would acquire a population of 78,000 almost overnight. Another plant sprang up at Hanford, Washing-

In broad-brimmed hat, J. Robert Oppenheimer, director of the Atomic Laboratories at Los Alamos, New Mexico, and Major General Leslie R. Groves, head of the top-secret Manhattan Project, stand at the base of the tower on which the first atom bomb was exploded in July 1945. The heat of the blast vaporized most of the 100-foot steel structure instantaneously.

ton, to produce plutonium—a hitherto-unknown element that had been discovered as a result of cyclotron experiments at the University of Chicago and that lent itself as readily to a chain reaction as U-235.

The actual construction of the bomb went on at a top-secret plant on an isolated mesa about 20 miles from Santa Fe, New Mexico. There, work was directed by J. Robert Oppenheimer, a blue-eyed lean-faced physicist in his early forties with a zest for knowledge that ranged from Sanskrit poetry to Marxist dialectics.

The amazing thing is that over the years the project's objective was known to scarcely a dozen people. Indeed, so well kept was the secret that when Roosevelt suddenly died of a cerebral hemorrhage on the afternoon of April 12, 1945, the Manhattan Project's existence was not even suspected by his Vice President and successor, Harry Truman. The new President was first informed of it on April 13 by Secretary of War Stimson. Admiral William D. Leahy, Chief of Staff to the President, could hardly believe what he heard. "That is the biggest fool thing we've ever done," he scoffed. "The bomb will never go off."

But by then the bomb was ready and the question of whether or not to use it would rest with the new President. Germany was already defeated and only a matter of days remained until it would surrender on May 7, 1945. But Japan was thought to have plenty of resistance left, and military and political leaders were pressing for a quick halt to the war in the Pacific. Truman left the decision pending and ordered a search for some alternative to dropping the bomb. Meanwhile, the bomb had yet to be tested.

The monumental test took place in a lonely New Mexico desert tract—aptly named *Jornada del Muerto,* or Journey of Death—at 5:29:45 a.m. on July 16, 1945. The results exceeded the expectations of even that small coterie sufficiently intimate with the undertaking to know what to look for. The bomb exploded with a brightness so great that its flash could have been seen from another planet; its temperature at the point of explosion was 100 million degrees Fahrenheit, four times that of the central core of the sun.

The effect was to be burned forever on the minds of those few who witnessed the occasion. It was "a sunrise such as the world had never seen, a great green supersun," wrote William L. Laurence of *The New York Times,* the only journalist present. "Up it went, a great ball of fire about a mile in diameter, changing colors as it kept shooting upward, from deep purple to orange, expanding, growing bigger, rising as it expanded, an elemental force freed from its bonds after being chained for billions of years." Continuing in a spirit of awed reverence, he concluded: "One felt as though one were present at the moment of creation when God said: 'Let there be light.'"

When the fire subsided, it left behind a great black cloud that drifted off in a form that some of the physicists present saw as a great symbolic question mark.

In the moment of explosion, the eerie light of the bomb was seen from a distance of 50 miles; tremors were felt as far away as 235 miles, and the only official explanation was a canned Army press release about the explosion of "an ammunition magazine." Hours later, a small dog in the scientists' base camp was found still shivering with terror in the blistering heat, the desert toads had not yet resumed singing and for miles around horses continued to whinny.

When the smoke cloud had dissipated and the scientists could move in on the site to examine it, they found that the steel tower cradling the bomb had vanished almost completely; the explosion had left a giant 1,200-foot-wide crater in the sand, which had solidified and turned jade-green. All animal and plant life had been destroyed within a radius of one mile.

Word of the test's results reached Truman in Potsdam, where he was attending his first conference as head of state with Churchill. The Prime Minister had been let in on the Manhattan Project by Roosevelt, but Premier Josef Stalin had not been. Truman casually conveyed to Stalin that the U.S. had "a new weapon of unusual destructive force." Stalin—who already had some inkling from his spy network—said simply that he hoped we would make "good use of it against the Japanese," Truman later recalled. Meanwhile, Truman's advisers had already reported to him that they could "see no acceptable alternative to direct military use." He took their advice and decided the bomb should be dropped on Japan.

Three weeks later that would be done. It would bring to an end the most devastating war in history, dealing the final blow with the most savage weapon man had ever devised. And the home front was to settle into peace.

THE COMMANDER IN CHIEF

AN ARISTOCRAT WITH A COMMON TOUCH

One-year-old Franklin perches on the shoulder of his father, James Roosevelt, in 1883. An only child, F.D.R. wore dresses until he was five.

When America's Commander in Chief, Franklin D. Roosevelt, returned to the U.S. from a war conference in Casablanca in 1943, Kansas editor William Allen White, who had bitterly opposed many of F.D.R.'s policies, paid his old enemy a tribute. "Biting nails—good, hard, bitter Republican nails," White wrote, "we are compelled to admit that Franklin Roosevelt is the most unaccountable and on the whole the most enemy-baffling President that this United States has ever seen. . . ."

Few people in American public life have evoked stronger emotions than Franklin Roosevelt. He was one of the most charming, adroit, self-assured and effective politicians that America has produced. Occupying the Presidency longer than any man in history—12 years 1 month 8 days—he steered the nation through two of the worst crises that it had faced since the terrible days of the Civil War: the Great Depression and World War II. For Americans during the War years, he was the President, Commander in Chief and a father figure rolled into one.

There was little in Roosevelt's background to suggest that he was equipped for such a demanding role or that he would gain such esteem. As a child, he was privileged and pampered. He grew up in a world of governesses, private tutors, dancing lessons, a pony named Debby and an overly protective mother. At eight, he wrote his father proudly, "Mama left this morning and I am going to take my bath alone." He was enrolled in elite schools—Groton and Harvard—and averaged a "gentleman's C." His college career was summed up in a line written to his mother: "Am doing a little studying, a little riding and a few party calls." He derived endless pleasure from his 21-foot sailboat and might well have resigned himself to a life of leisure.

But there was something in Roosevelt that would not settle for a life of ease. Partly it was his own restless ambition and partly it was the challenge imposed on him early in his career by the illness that left his legs paralyzed. Partly also, it lay with the fact that he was a born politician—an aristocrat with a common touch.

Dressed in the sailor suit he hated, young Franklin (top, right) and one of his cousins tussle with the wheel of his father's yacht in the 1880s. His boyhood sailing trips to the family's summer home on Campobello Island in New Brunswick, kindled a lifelong love for ships and the sea. After F.D.R. became engaged to Eleanor Roosevelt (right), who was his fifth cousin once removed, the couple spent a closely chaperoned vacation at the resort. At their wedding ceremony held on Saint Patrick's Day in 1905, President Theodore Roosevelt gave the bride, his niece, in marriage.

n the summer of 1926, F.D.R. was treated by Dr. William MacDonald (on he right) at Marion, Massachusetts. Each day he spent several hours exercising on a "walking board" in an attempt to restore his leg muscles.

Leaning on a cane, Governor Roosevelt talks nose to nose with Reuben Appel, a Hyde Park, New York, neighbor. F.D.R. took to the streets often to gauge the mood of the people he called "Mr. and Mrs. Average Voter."

With his boss, Navy Secretary Josephus Daniels, Franklin Roosevelt s photographed at the Navy Department in Washington in 1917. Daniels, vho was a homespun editor-politician from the South, was the only dministrative superior Roosevelt ever had during his political career.

YEARS OF PROMISE, TRAGEDY AND TRIUMPH

Roosevelt was a brash young state sena-or and delegate to the 1912 Democratic National Convention in Baltimore when ne met Josephus Daniels, a Woodrow Wil-son supporter from North Carolina, who vas so captivated by F.D.R. that he later described the encounter as "love at first sight." Appointed Secretary of the Navy by Wilson in 1913, Daniels picked the young New Yorker as his Assistant Secretary.

Roosevelt delighted in the job. He liked he 17-gun salutes fired in his honor, be-ame an advocate of a greatly strength

ened Navy and, by 1916, was urging the Administration to discard its policy of neu-trality and get into World War I. During his seven years in Washington, F.D.R. so im-pressed Democratic Party chieftains that he was named James M. Cox's running mate in the losing 1920 Presidential cam-paign against Warren G. Harding.

Handsome, able and articulate, his fu-ture seemed unlimited in spite of the lost election. But on August 10, 1921, while sailing at Campobello Island, he sighted a small brush fire and put ashore to help fight it. Later, he took a swim in a chilly lake, then ran a mile and a half home in a wet bathing suit. The next morning he woke with a high fever and felt pains in his

back and legs. Soon his legs were com-pletely paralyzed. The diagnosis was polic

Following a strict regimen of physica therapy, Roosevelt exercised long and hard and went to Warm Springs, Georgia, fo further treatment. But despite his efforts he was never again able to walk unaided "Not one man in ten millions," wrote Win-ston Churchill years later, "would have at-tempted to plunge into a life of physica and mental exertion and of hard, ceaseless political controversy." But Roosevelt was determined to make the plunge. He wen back to work—in a New York City law firm—and in 1928 propelled himself into the forefront of national politics by win-ning the governorship of New York

HOURS OF CRISIS AT HOME AND ABROAD

After serving two terms as Governor of New York, F.D.R. was nominated for President on the Democratic ticket in 1932. He campaigned in 41 states and won a land-slide victory over Herbert Hoover.

The Presidency seemed tailor made for a man with Roosevelt's zest for political combat. "There is nothing I love as much as a good fight," he once said. He enjoyed jousting with recalcitrant Republicans and dissident Democrats, haggling with Congress over legislation and matching wits with reporters in his press conferences.

He was preoccupied in the early years of his White House tenure with emergency measures to rally the nation from the paralyzing effects of the Great Depression. But by the mid-1930s, F.D.R.'s attention turned more and more to foreign affairs. "I am very much more worried about the world situation than about the domestic," he told a friend in 1935. And as the war clouds gathered in Europe, there never was any doubt in his mind about the magnitude of the threat to the U.S. "There comes a time in the affairs of men when they must prepare to defend, not their homes alone but the tenets of faith and humanity on which their churches, their governments and their very civilization are founded," he said.

Gradually, in spite of determined opposition, he edged the U.S. toward active participation on the side of the Allies. "I am almost literally walking on eggs," he said. Buffeting a heavy tide of isolationism, he called for a "quarantine" of the aggressors as early as 1937, secured the passage of Lend-Lease to Britain in late 1941, and arranged for the transfer of 50 U.S. destroyers to the British at the height of the Battle of the Atlantic in early 1940.

A jaunty F.D.R. spars with reporters after a Fourth of July picnic on the lawn at Hyde Park in 1939.

The President carves Thanksgiving turkey for Mrs. Roosevelt and the patients at Warm Springs in 1938.

The President clutches a railing as he leaves the Capitol after warning Congress in 1939 of aggression abroad and urging higher defense spending at home.

President Roosevelt chats with two midgets during a ride down the half-mile-long assembly line at the Willow Run, Michigan, bomber plant in September 1942. Because of their size, midgets could work in cramped spaces in airplane wings. During the War, F.D.R. made several tours of the U.S. to spur production, inspect military bases and boost morale.

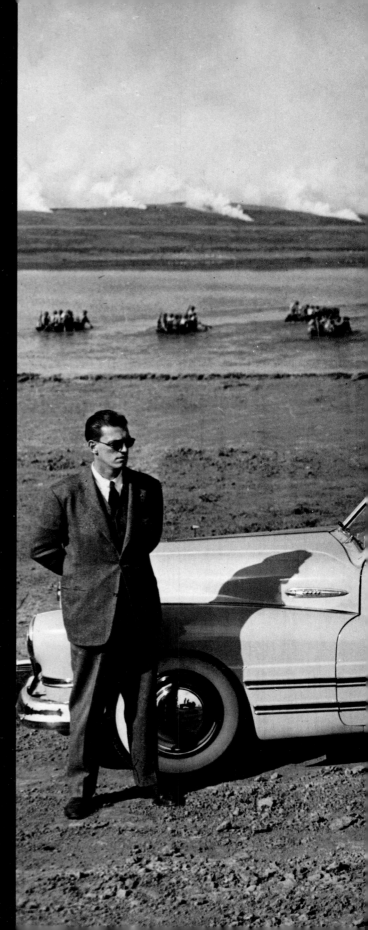

From a vantage point in the front seat of his open limousine, F.D.R. watches a staged amphibious landing at a lake at Camp Carson, Colorado, in 1943. The Commander in Chief enjoyed meeting GIs and in that same year, while attending the Casablanca Conference, he took time to visit the troops, the first President since Lincoln to do so in an active theater of war.

F.D.R. awards a posthumous Congressional Medal of Honor to the widow and son of Colonel Demas T. Craw, killed while attempting to arrange a truce during Allied landings in French North Africa in November 1942.

Dressed in a dinner jacket and a black tie, F.D.R. keeps in touch with the nation by radio. The gala setting—the East Room of the White House during a diplomatic reception—was unusual for a "fireside chat."

Gathered with his neighbors on election night in 1944, the President, wearing the Navy cape he preferred to an overcoat, watches a torchlight victory celebration from the porch of his Hyde Park home. Enjoying the spectacle with him are Mrs. Roosevelt, daughter Anna and Elmer von Wagner, a longtime political friend who helped produce the festivities.

The drawn visages of Churchill and Roosevelt reflect the tension of years of war leadership at the second Quebec Conference in September 1944.

A haggard Roosevelt talks with Stalin's deputy, Foreign Minister Vyacheslav Molotov (in fur cap) and Churchill (center rear) at Yalta early in 1945.

BONE-WEARYING
WARTIME MEETINGS

In the pursuit of his wartime duties, Roosevelt went to any lengths necessary to meet with Allied leaders. He journeyed to such distant places as Quebec, Casablanca and Cairo to confer with Prime Minister Winton Churchill. And he went to Teheran and Yalta for discussions with Churchill and Russian Premier Josef Stalin.

Roosevelt and Churchill hit it off from the start. "It's fun to be in the same decade with you," Roosevelt cabled "Winnie" in 1941. Churchill said being with F.D.R. was "like opening a bottle of champagne." The two Western leaders were split on Stalin. F.D.R. said he "got along fine" with the Russian leader, but Churchill regarded him with suspicion.

Roosevelt's travels were bone-wearying, and he usually visited Warm Springs, Georgia, after his return home to recoup his strength. But by the time he went to Yalta in 1945 the War years had taken their toll. "I noticed that the President was ailing," Churchill later commented. "Often there was a far-away look in his eyes." His jaw sagged; the famous cigarette holder dangled. Soon he was back at Warm Springs, but this time it was too late. On the 12th of April, 1945, while posing for his portrait, the President succumbed to a massive cerebral hemorrhage.

A DAY OF NATIONAL SORROW

Franklin Roosevelt was such a familiar figure and was so much a part of the lives of all Americans that the news of his death struck almost everyone on the home front with the same impact as the loss of a member of the family. A shopkeeper in Pittsburgh closed up and hung a hand-lettered sign in the window: "He died." In New York a taxi driver got out of his cab, sat down on the curb and wept. "It doesn't seem possible," said a woman in Detroit. "It seems to me that he will be back on the radio tomorrow, reassuring us that it was just a mistake." In Washington, a soldier spoke the nation's grief: "I felt as if I knew him. I felt as if he knew me—and I felt as if he liked me."

A special train bore the President's body north to Washington. All along the route, Americans gathered to say farewell. At the White House, the coffin lay in the East Room, where at the close of another terrible war, almost 80 years to the day, Abraham Lincoln's body had lain. In a steady downpour, the train traveled the last leg of the journey to Hyde Park, where the wartime leader was given a solemn military funeral. "All that is within me cries to go back to my home on the Hudson River," F.D.R. had said nine months before. At long last, he was home.

In the garden near the house where he was born 63 years earlier, Franklin Roosevelt is

202

laid to rest by an honor guard of soldiers, sailors and Marines. As workmen began filling the grave, a lone figure returned to watch. It was Eleanor Roosevelt

BIBLIOGRAPHY

Adams, Henry H., *Harry Hopkins*. G. P. Putnam's Sons, 1977.

Ayer, Fred, Jr., *Before the Colors Fade: Portrait of a Soldier, George S. Patton, Jr.* Houghton Mifflin Co., 1964.

Ayling, Keith, *Calling All Women*. Harper & Brothers, 1942.

Barnes, G. M., *Weapons of World War II*. D. Van Nostrand Co., 1947.

Baxandall, Rosalyn, Linda Gordon and Susan Reverby, eds., *America's Working Women*. Random House, 1976.

Baxter, James Phinney III, *Scientists against Time*. M.I.T. Press, 1946.

Bliss, Edward, Jr., ed., *In Search of Light*. Alfred A. Knopf, 1967.

Blum, John Morton, *V Was for Victory: Politics and American Culture during World War II*. Harcourt Brace Jovanovich, 1976.

Burns, James MacGregor:
   Roosevelt: The Lion and the Fox. Harcourt, Brace & World, 1956.
   Roosevelt: The Soldier of Freedom. Harcourt Brace Jovanovich, 1970.

Carr, Lowell Juilliard, and James Edson Sturmer, *Willow Run: Study of Industrialization and Cultural Inadequacy*. Harper, 1952.

Catton, Bruce, *The War Lords of Washington*. Harcourt, Brace & Co., 1948.

Cerf, Bennett, *Try & Stop Me. A Collection of Anecdotes and Stories, Mostly Humorous*. Garden City Publishing Co., Inc., 1944.

Chase, William Henry, *The American Woman: Her Changing Social, Economic and Political Roles, 1920-1970*. Oxford University Press, 1972.

Churchill, Winston S., *The Grand Alliance*. Bantam, 1950.

Clark, Ronald W., *The Birth of the Bomb*. Phoenix House Ltd., 1961.

Cochran, Bert, *Harry Truman and the Crisis Presidency*. Funk and Wagnalls, 1973.

Colby, Benjamin, *'Twas a Famous Victory: Deceptions and Propaganda in the War with Germany*. Arlington House, 1974.

Conrat, Maisie and Richard, *Executive Order 9066*. M.I.T. Press, 1972.

Cooper, Martin R., Glen T. Barton and Albert P. Brodell, *Progress of Farm Mechanization*. Miscellaneous Publications #630, U.S. Dept. of Agriculture, 1947.

Correspondents of TIME, LIFE and FORTUNE, The, *December 7: The First Thirty Hours*. Alfred A. Knopf, 1942.

Dalfiume, Richard M., *Desegregation of the U.S. Armed Forces*. University of Missouri Press, 1969.

Daniels, Roger, *Concentration Camps, USA: Japanese Americans & World War II*. Dryden Press, 1971.

Davis, Forrest, and Ernest K. Lindley, *How War Came*. Simon and Schuster, 1942.

Fowler, Gene, *Good Night, Sweet Prince*. Viking Press, 1944.

Garraty, John A., *The American Nation: A History of the United States*. Harper & Row, Publishers, Inc., and American Heritage Publishers, 1966.

Girdner, Audrie, and Anne Loftis, *The Great Betrayal*. The Macmillan Co., 1969.

Goodman, Jack, ed., *While You Were Gone*. Da Capo Press, 1974.

Groueff, Stephane, *Manhattan Project: The Untold Story of the Making of the Atomic Bomb*. Little, Brown and Co., 1967.

Guiles, Fred Lawrence, *Norma Jean: The Life of Marilyn Monroe*. McGraw-Hill Book Co., 1969.

Gunther, John:
   Inside U.S.A. Harper & Brothers, 1947.
   Roosevelt in Retrospect. Harper & Brothers, 1950.

Hargrove, Marion, *See Here, Private Hargrove*. Henry Holt and Co., 1942.

Hinshaw, David, *The Home Front*. G. P. Putnam's Sons, 1943.

Hoehling, A. A.:
   Home Front, U.S.A. Thomas Y. Crowell, 1966.
   The Week before Pearl Harbor. W. W. Norton, 1963.

Hosokawa, Bill, *Nisei*. William Morrow, 1969.

Lamont, Lansing, *Day of Trinity*. Atheneum, 1965.

Langer, William L., and S. Everett Gleason, *The Undeclared War, 1940-1941*. Harper & Brothers Publishers, 1953.

Laurence, William L., *Men and Atoms: The Discovery, the Uses and the Future of Atomic Energy*. Simon and Schuster, 1959.

Lingeman, Richard R., *Don't You Know There's a War On?* G. P. Putnam's Sons, 1970.

Lord, Walter, *Day of Infamy*. Bantam, 1957.

Manchester, William, *The Glory and the Dream*. Bantam, 1973.

Martin, Joe, *My First Fifty Years in Politics*. McGraw-Hill Book Co., 1960.

Martin, Pete, *Will Acting Spoil Marilyn Monroe?* Doubleday & Co., 1956.

Meyer, Agnes E., *Journey through Chaos*. Harcourt, Brace & Co., 1944.

Miller, Merle, *Plain Speaking: An Oral Biography of Harry S. Truman*. Berkley Publishing Corp., 1974.

Morison, Samuel Eliot, *The Rising Sun in the Pacific*. Little, Brown and Co., 1948.

Morris, Joe Alex, *Deadline Every Minute*. Doubleday & Co., Inc., 1957.

Nelson, Donald M., *Arsenal of Democracy: The Story of American War Production*. Da Capo Press, 1973.

Nesbitt, Henrietta, *White House Diary*. Doubleday & Co., 1948.

Pendleton, Ann, *Hit the River, Sister*. Howell Suskin, 1943.

Penfold, J. B., "Japan's Rambling Balloon Barrage." Published in U.S. Naval Institute Proceedings, Vol. 73, August 1947.

Perrett, Geoffrey, *Days of Sadness, Years of Triumph*. Coward, McCann & Geoghegan, 1973.

Phillips, Cabell, *The 1940s*. The Macmillan Co., 1975.

Pinza, Ezio, *Ezio Pinza*. Rinehart, 1958.

Pogue, Forrest C., *George C. Marshall: Ordeal and Hope*. Viking Press, 1965.

Polenberg, Richard:
   ed., *America at War*. Prentice-Hall, 1968.
   War and Society. J. B. Lippincott, 1972.

Pusey, Merlo J., *Big Government: Can We Control It?* Harper & Brothers Publishers, 1948.

Rachlis, Eugene, *They Came to Kill*. Random House, 1961.

Reilly, Michael F., and William J. Slocum, *Reilly of the White House*. Simon and Schuster, 1947.

Rogers, Donald I., *Since You Went Away*. Arlington House, 1973.

Roosevelt, Eleanor, *This I Remember*. Harper & Brothers, 1949.

Roskill, S. W., *The War at Sea*. Her Majesty's Stationery Office, 1956.

Shea, Naney, *The Waacs*. Harper & Brothers, 1943.

Sherwin, Martin J., *A World Destroyed: The Atomic Bomb and the Grand Alliance*. Alfred A. Knopf, 1975.

Sherwood, Robert E., *Roosevelt and Hopkins*. Harper & Brothers, 1948.

tenBroek, Jacobus, Edward N. Barnhart and Floyd W. Matson, *Prejudice, War and the Constitution*. University of California Press, 1968.

Thomson, Harry C., and Lida Mayo, *United States Army in World War II: The Technical Services. The Ordnance Department: Procurement and Supply*. Dept. of the Army, 1960.

Toland, John, *The Rising Sun*. Random House, 1970.

Treadwell, Mattie E., *The Women's Army Corps*. Dept. of the Army, 1953.

Truman, Harry S., *Memoirs by Harry S. Truman, Vol. I: Years of Decisions*. Doubleday & Co., 1955.

Tully, Grace, *F.D.R. My Boss*. Charles Scribner's Sons, 1949.

U.S. Air Force Historical Aircraft Background Information. Secretary of the Air Force, Office of Information, Internal Information Division, 1970.

von Miklos, Josephine, *I Took a War Job*. Simon and Schuster, 1943.

Walton, Francis, *Miracle of World War II: How American Industry Made Victory Possible*. The Macmillan Co., 1956.

Warner, William L., *Democracy in Jonesville*. Greenwood Press, 1976.

Webber, Bert, *Retaliation: Japanese Attacks and Allied Countermeasures on the Pacific Coast in World War II*. University of Oregon Press, 1975.

West, J. B., *Upstairs at the White House*. Coward, McCann & Geoghegan, 1973.

Whitehead, Don, *The FBI Story*. Random House, 1956.

Wittner, Lawrence S., *Rebels against War: The American Peace Movement*. Columbia University Press, 1969.

Wynn, Neil A., *The Afro-American and the Second World War*. Paul Elek, 1976.

Zolotow, Maurice, *Marilyn Monroe*. Harcourt, Brace & Co., 1960.

ACKNOWLEDGMENTS

The index for this book was prepared by Mel Ingber. For help given in the preparation of this book the editors wish to express their gratitude to Clarence Boston, Records Manager, U.S. Selective Service System, Washington, D.C.; David Bruster, Historian, Agricultural History Group, Economic Research Service, U.S. Department of Agriculture, Washington, D.C.; George Coffman, Agricultural Economist, Economic Research Service, U.S. Department of Agriculture, Washington, D.C.; V. M. Destefano, Chief, Reference Branch, U.S. Army Audiovisual Division, Pentagon, Washington, D.C.; Detmar H. Finke, Historian, Center of Military History, Department of the Army, Washington, D.C.; Robert Fredlund, Director of Administrative Programs, U.S. Treasury Department, Washington, D.C.; Jerry Hill, Industrial and Social Branch, National Archives, Washington, D.C.; James Idema, Washington, D.C.; Francis X. Maloney, Assistant Director, Boston Public Library, Boston, Massachusetts; Colonel Bettie J. Morden, Center of Military History, Department of the Army, Washington, D.C.; Allan Priaux, King Features Syndicate, New York, New York; James Sullivan, Cedar Falls, Iowa; Clarence Taylor, Houston, Texas.

INDEX

Numerals in italics indicate an illustration
of the subject mentioned.